Copyright Law On Campus

Marc Lindsey

WSU PRESS

Washington State University Press
Pullman, Washington

WASHINGTON STATE
UNIVERSITY

Washington State University Press
PO Box 645910
Pullman, Washington 99164-5910
Phone: 800-354-7360
Fax: 509-335-8568
E-mail: wsupress@wsu.edu
Web site: wsupress.wsu.edu

Library of Congress Cataloging-in-Publication Data

Lindsey, Marc.
  Copyright law on campus / Marc Lindsey.
     p. cm.
  ISBN 0-87422-264-8 (pbk. : alk. paper)
     1. Fair use (Copyright)—United States. 2. Public domain (Copyright law)—United States.
  3. Copyright—Electronic information resources—United States. I. Title.

KF3030.1.L56 2003
346.7304'82--dc21   2003000566

WSU PRESS
Fine Quality Books from the Pacific Northwest

Table of Contents

Preface v

Chapter One: The Source and Nature of Copyright Law.. 1
    a. A Brief History
    b. Exclusive Rights of Copyright
    c. Nature of Works Protected
    d. Legal Procedures
    e. Important Reasons to Register a Copyright
    f. The Copyright Notice
    g. Work-for-Hire Doctrine

Chapter Two: Duration of Copyrights and Public Domain 6
    a. Duration and the Complex Life Span of Copyrights
    b. Public Domain
    c. The Erosion of Public Domain and the Tug-of-War Behind Legislation

Chapter Three: Copyright Infringement Lawsuits—The Risk of Infringing 9
    a. The Chain of Liability
    b. Actual or Statutory Damages
    c. Criminal Offenses
    d. Attorneys' Fees
    e. Mitigating the Risk

Chapter Four: Getting Permission 12
    a. Copyright Clearance Center
    b. Permission from the Author or Publisher
    c. Permission for Photographs or Images
    d. Permission to Play Music in Public

Chapter Five: The Mystic Doctrine of Fair Use 16
    a. Controversial Nature and Purpose
    b. The Federal Statute: 17 U.S.C. Section 107
    c. The Four Factors of Fair Use
    d Analyzing the Four Factors
    e. Applying the Facts
    f. Fair Use Exercises
    g. Classroom Guidelines
    h. Fair Use Analysis Choices

Chapter Six: Copyright Law and the Internet 29
    a. Whose Laws, Whose Courts Apply?
    b. Uploading Visual Images: Thumbnail Images
    c. Copying "FAQs" from a Web Site
    d. Deep Linking
    e. Digital Millennium Copyright Act
    f. Common Internet Copyright Issues on Campus

Chapter Seven: Copyright and Distance Education 35
    a. What the TEACH Act Permits
    b. Exceptions, Limitations, and Conditions

Chapter Eight: Copyright Policies on Campus 38
    a. Copyright Infringement and Plagiarism
    b. A Comparison of Copyright Web Sites
    c. Sovereign Immunity and Ethics
    d. Resistance to Promoting Fair Use
    e. Time to Address Change

Appendix A: When Unpublished and Published Works Pass into the Public Domain 43

Appendix B: Public Domain Sources 45

Appendix C: Classroom Guidelines 49

Appendix D: TEACH Act Checklist 51

Appendix E: Proposed Graduate Program Copyright Guidelines 53

Preface

Only one thing is impossible for God: to find any sense in the copyright law on this planet.
—Mark Twain, Notebook 1903

Sharing information is the fundamental nature of education. Restricting the sharing of information is the fundamental nature of copyright law. There is an exception in this law to accommodate education and other exercises of the First Amendment right to free speech. This exception is known as the Fair Use Doctrine. But no one can seem to agree where fair use begins or ends. In the words of a federal appellate judge applying the copyright law in the context of higher education, "Fair Use is one of the most unsettled areas of the law. The doctrine has been said to be so flexible as virtually to defy definition." (*Princeton University Press v. Michigan Document Services, Inc.*) Participants of higher education are stuck with a concept that defies safe harbor guidelines for determining what is right or wrong in the collection and dissemination of information—the very means of teaching students.

We cannot wait for the courts or the legislatures to sort this out. We are the education system, so let's ply our trade and teach ourselves! Why not learn what we can, what is practical, and what enables us to devise a reasonable medium—fair to publishers and fair to educators. Let's learn about copyright law, or at least enough to educate administrators and faculty and, in turn, the students who stand to face these issues not only in school, but in life. What information are we restricted from? What information do

we need permission to copy? How do we get permission? What kind of use of information is "fair use," so we don't need permission? How do we determine it as such?

The approach in this book is to explain the basics of copyright law in terms relevant to higher education. Hopefully, the knowledge can be used to strike a fair medium between the rights of copyright owners and those engaged in giving and receiving a meaningful education. The book explains how to acquire permission when it appears legally prudent to do so. There are also suggestions for how to apply the Fair Use Doctrine when circumstances make obtaining permission prohibitive. The best interest of education requires a copyright policy that is more accessible than the conflicting analyses of the federal courts. This is a studied attempt at just such a policy.

The focus of this book is limited to the most frequently encountered copyright issues affecting college campuses, while avoiding the depth of subject and case law history that would be presented to law students. The goal is to keep the subject as uncomplicated and engaging as possible, without miring the reader in needless legal detail. The principal objectives are to provide, for as diverse an audience as possible, an elementary understanding of basic copyright law and fair use, and to provide guidelines for application.

Chapter One

The Source and Nature of Copyright Law

The Congress shall have Power… to Promote the Progress of Science and useful Arts, by securing for limited Times to Authors and Inventors the exclusive Right to their respective Writings and Discoveries.
—(I U.S.C. Const. Art. 1, Section 8, clause 8.)

A Brief History

The first copyright statute in the United States was enacted in 1790. The Constitution directs Congress to make laws to promote the arts and sciences by giving artists and authors the exclusive rights to their work.

At the time the Constitution was drafted in the late 1700s, the Founding Fathers recognized the historic struggle between the creators of art, music, and other original works and the publishing industry that then exploited those works for economic gain. For example, even Wolfgang Amadeus Mozart, one of the most brilliant musicians of all time, lived and died virtually destitute and was buried in a pauper's grave. Before the enactment of any legal protections, others could copy an artist's work freely, either to enjoy themselves or to sell to others without due recognition or remuneration given to the originator. The resulting economic dynamics affected both the quantity and quality of art produced.

With the invention of the printing press, the world was confronted with two new problems. First, governments were unable to control the quantity and content of the reading matter available to the public. And second, literary "pirates" appeared who would copy the works of writers without paying them and sometimes without even giving them credit. After copying the artists' work without permission, these profiteers would then sell the work to the public at a lower price than the legal edition and undercut the original market for new creative works.

The early solution in England was to give the Stationer's Guild, the publishing industry, a legal monopoly in return for a certain degree of censorship over ideas to which the Crown was opposed. However, this arrangement gave the publishing monopolies too much power, and, in 1710, the English Parliament enacted the Statute of Anne, which for the first time vested a "copy right" in the author of a work.[1]

As the American Founding Fathers sought to balance the sometimes competing needs of creators, publishers, and distributors in such a way that knowledge and creative works would be widely disseminated, they were strongly influenced by the principles first established in the Statute of Anne. They hoped that by protecting the author's copyright, writers would enjoy the fruits and fame of their works. The United States Copyright Law is based on a utilitarian incentive: by giving authors and artists the exclusive right to exploit their creative works, they would be motivated to produce better art and more of it.[2]

Exclusive Rights of Copyright

Copyright law gives artists, authors and musicians the exclusive right, or sole right, to:
- Copy their works
- Prepare derivatives or revisions of their works
- Distribute or publish their works
- Perform or display their works in public[3]

Nature of Works Protected

❖ What Is Protected by Copyright? Is There a Minimum Standard of Art Required?

As "beauty is in the eye of the beholder," there is no minimum artistic standard. As once stated by a judge in a copyright case, "individual perception of the beautiful is too varied a power to permit a narrow or rigid concept of art."[4] However, works must be original and not the work of another artist. Works must also be "fixed in any tangible medium of expression, now known or later developed, from which they can be perceived, reproduced or otherwise communicated, either directly or with the aid of a machine or device."[5] Another way to look at it: a work of art, writing, or music must be recorded in a way that can be understood by someone other than the author. The copyright statute cites these examples of work protected by copyright:

- Literary works
- Musical works, including any accompanying words
- Dramatic works, including any accompanying music
- Pantomimes and choreographic works
- Pictorial, graphic, and sculptural works
- Motion pictures and audiovisual works
- Sound recordings
- Architectural works

These categories of copyright-protected works are by no means exclusive. Photographs are protected.[6] The drawing of cartoons is protected by copyright and trademark law.[7] What about the simple finger painting of a young child? An email to a co-worker? An idea for a novel scribbled on a cocktail napkin? These are all protected by copyright. If you can see, hear, smell, or touch any expression of an idea that is an original work, it is highly likely that it is protected by copyright law.

❖ What Is Not Protected by Copyright?

Copyright does not protect unexpressed ideas, procedure, process, system, method of operation, concept, principle, or discovery.[8] The term "discovery" refers to such things as historical and scientific facts. For example, a movie about dinosaurs does not infringe the copyrights of *Jurassic Park,* in and of itself. A television show about a fast-draw gun battle on Main Street does not infringe the copyrights of *Gunsmoke.* However it is important to distinguish between discovered facts and the *expression* of those facts. For example, let's say an astronomer discovered the near-miss of earth by an asteroid. A newspaper reporter writes an article about the incident. Another newspaper reporter reads the article and writes an article for his newspaper. Is the copyright to the first article infringed? It depends on how the second article was expressed. If it was substantially similar to the wording, phrasing, and composition of the first article, then a court might find it to be copyright infringement. A finding of no infringement may occur if the court found that the second reporter merely reported on the same incident, but expressed the incident in an original way. The discovery of the asteroid by itself is not protected by copyright. Copyright law Professor Melville Nimmer put it this way:

The "discoverer" of a scientific fact as to the nature of the physical world, an historic fact, a contemporary news event, or any other "fact," may not claim to be the "author" of that fact. If anyone may claim authorship of facts, it must be the Supreme Author of us all. The discoverer merely finds and records. He may not claim that facts are "original" to him, although there may be originality and hence authorship in the manner of reporting, i.e., the "expression" of the facts. Since copyright may only be conferred upon "authors," it follows that quite apart from their status as "ideas," discoveries as facts per se may not be the subject of copyright.[9]

Another scenario in which copyright issues can be confusing is when something is spoken by one person and recorded by someone else. Bear in mind that works must be fixed to a tangible medium to be protected. In the case of *Hemingway vs. Random House,*[10] following the death of author Ernest Hemingway, his widow, Mary Hemingway, filed a lawsuit against publisher Random House for the infringement of copyright to conversations Hemingway had, usually at a bar, with his friend A. E. Hotchner. Ms. Hemingway claimed that the lengthy verbatim quotes that appeared in Hotchner's book published by Random House, *Papa Hemingway,* were the property of Hemingway's estate and as such their unauthorized publication was an infringement of copyright. The court deciding the case found evidence that, regardless where copyright begins and ends, Hemingway's conduct implied his consent for Hotchner to record and publish the conversations. There is still very little other precedent on this issue which, like so many other copyright issues, remains ripe for judicial interpretation.

Surfacing recently has been the question of whether copyright protects speech in classrooms. Are the spoken lectures of professors protected from students who tape-record, publish, and sell transcripts of the lectures to other students? There are court cases pending in California against certain Internet companies that published class lecture transcripts online after hiring students to tape-record the lectures. Predicting how the courts may rule on this issue is precarious at best. Copyright specialists seem to be divided as to whether or not lectures—as content delivered verbally—are protected or not. One sensible theory is that copyright could protect lectures as performances of outlines authored by the professors. Since their work is fixed in the tangible medium of an outline or syllabus it would thus be protected. If a lecture can be considered a "performance" of an outline or syllabus, then the professor has the exclusive right to "perform" the work publicly. While an idea expressed only verbally may not be protected, a verbal presentation made from a written outline might be.

Legal Procedures

It used to be necessary to register works through the U.S. Copyright Office, in the Library of Congress, in order to secure copyright protection. Later, it was sufficient to post a copyright notice on the work—i.e., name, year, and the word "copyright" or the symbol, ©. If these formalities were not observed, with certain statutory exceptions, the copyright would expire and fall into the "Public Domain," making the work available for anyone to copy without obtaining permission.

Under current law, an author need not comply with any formal procedures in order to receive copyright protection. Copyright protection springs into existence the moment a work is recorded or fixed in a tangible medium. For example, the moment words are typed or written on paper, or music recorded or "scored" on sheet music, it is protected by copyright. The moment a painter's brush makes contact with a canvas, exclusive rights to the painting are in force. After a photograph is snapped, no one may copy it without the photographer's permission.

Important Reasons to Register a Copyright

While it is no longer necessary to comply with registration formalities in order for a work to be protected by copyright, compliance can make the difference between winning or losing an infringement case in court. Because the U.S. Copyright Law is a federal law, enforcement of copyrights takes place in federal court. The copyright for a work must be registered in the U.S. Copyright Office before a lawsuit can even be filed in federal court.[11] There is another important reason to register copyright: to officially document the creator of a work and its date of origin. Often, in infringement suits, the principal issue revolves around who first created the work in question. In many copyright cases, contested works often are not registered until just prior to filing an infringement lawsuit. Although registration is no longer a prerequisite for copyright protection, it is recommended as a prudent legal strategy.

Registering copyrights is also a prerequisite to recovering attorney's fees. In an infringement lawsuit, the judge has the discretion to make the losing party pay a "reasonable fee" for the opponent's attorney.[12] In order for a copyright holder to be awarded compensation for attorney's fees in the event of an infringement lawsuit, it must be shown that copyright was registered within three months of publication.[13] If a work has been infringed before it was published, it is necessary to indicate that the

copyright was registered before it was infringed.

Registering copyright is easy, relatively inexpensive, and can be performed online or by mail. Depending on the work to be registered, a particular form must be completed. To request a registration form, the U.S. Copyright Office may be contacted at (202) 707-3000. Examples of form categories include:

- Form TX, for a "non-dramatic literary work";
- Form PA, for "performing arts," including songs, movies, or scripts for dramatic plays;
- Form VA, for a photograph or any graphic art.

The U.S. Copyright Office can also be contacted for information online at: **http://www.copyright.gov/**.

Filing fees and forms change from time to time; it is advisable to research the forms and fees required by the U.S. Copyright Office before sending in an application for registration.

The Copyright Notice

Under the old Copyright Act of 1909, works lost copyright protection if published without the copyright notice. Copyright notice is disclosure of the name of the author, the year the work was created, and the word "copyright," or its abbreviation, or the symbol, ©. For all works created under the new Copyright Act of 1976, or on or after the date of January 1, 1978, it is not necessary to post a copyright notice. However, it is a good idea to always provide a copyright notice to notify the public of your claim. If it were necessary to file a lawsuit for infringement and the defendant proved that the infringement was innocent because the creator did not provide a copyright notice, the court might drastically reduce the recovery of damages awarded.[14]

Work-for-Hire Doctrine

Any works created by employees in the course of their employment are protected by the employer's copy-

right.[15] The only way an employee can retain his own copyright of works created on the job is by written agreement with his employer. The agreement must explicitly assign the employer's copyright to the employee to be legally effective. To be considered as work-for-hire, an employee must fit the description of a traditional employee: the employee's taxes and social security are withheld by the employer; he works under some supervision or direction, no matter how limited, of the employer; most of the primary tools for carrying out the tasks of employment are supplied by the employer; the employee generally works in a facility provided by the employer. Works that are created on an employee's own time and resources are not considered work for hire; therefore, an employee owns the copyrights to work created on his own time.

If contract labor or services are purchased, they are not considered legally as work-for-hire. Hence, contractors retain their own copyrights. In general, contractors pay their own payroll and taxes. They also usually use and provide their own supplies and work in their own facilities. If the contractor's customer desires to hold the copyrights of works that the contractor creates under the employment contract, the contractor must sign a written assignment of copyrights.

On college campuses, the policies that are in force may change the result, but not the legal effect, of work-for-hire. For example, many colleges maintain a policy that faculty may retain copyright to all work performed on the job, with exceptions such as software development or other work involving substantial college resources. However, since this can only be accomplished legally by a written agreement, copyright to the work is actually still held by the employing institution unless there is a signed agreement transferring copyright to the employee—*regardless of administrative policy or procedural precedence*. Although in practice few colleges make infringement claims against faculty, the safest approach for academic employees desiring to own the copyright to their work is to obtain a copyright transfer agreement in writing from their employing institution.

Students, unless they are creating works in the employ of the institution, own the copyright to all their own work done inside or outside the classroom. The copyright issue arises when faculty desire to make copies of student work, such as term papers or other assignments, for instructional purposes. The vast majority of students freely permit this use of their material, but, if they object, copyright law is on their side. To avoid a potential infringement in this area, faculty members should obtain written assignments of copyright or other written permission from students enrolled in their classes before copying student material.

Notes

1. 8 Anne ch. 19 (1710)
2. A good brief source for this information is: Edward Samuels, *The Illustrated Story of Copyright*, St. Martin's Press, NY; 2000, pp. 11–16. Or, in more detail: William F. Patry, *Copyright Law and Practice*, BNA, Salem, MA, pp. 3–36.
3. 17 USC Section 106
4. *Mazer vs. Stein, 347 U.S. 201(1954)*, at p. *214*
5. 17 USC Section 102(a)
6. *Burrow-Giles Lithographic Co. vs. Sarony*, 111 U. S. 53(1884)
7. *Walt Disney Productions vs. The Air Pirates*, 581 F.2d 751(9th Cir. 1978)
8. 17 USC Section 102(b)
9. Nimmer, *The Subject Matter of Copyright Under the Act of 1976, UCLA L. REV.978,1015-16(1977)(footnotes omitted)*
10. 23 N.Y. 2d 341 (Court of Appeals of New York 1969)
11. 17 USC Section 411(a)
12. 17 USC Section 505
13. 17 USC Section 412
14. 17 USC Section 405(b)
15. 17 USC Section 101

Chapter Two

Duration of Copyrights and Public Domain

Duration and the Complex Life Span of Copyrights

Duration of copyrights is helplessly fragmented by a long succession of various laws and statutes. For works created on or after January 1, 1978, the duration is the life of the author or artist plus 70 years.[1] If the work was created by a corporation, employee, or created anonymously or pseudonymously, the duration would be either 95 years from the date of publication, or 120 years from the date of creation, whichever was shorter.[2] Before January 1, 1978, the duration depended on which law existed at the time the work was created, whether or not the work was published, and whether or not the work was published with a copyright notice. Appendix A gives a listing of copyright expirations assigned before and after January 1, 1978.[3] It's helpful to remember one simple rule of thumb: copyright has expired on all works dated before 1923. They have entered the "public domain," and as such are free to be copied by anyone at any time.

> *Copyright has expired on all works dated before 1923.*

While copyright protection endures, you may not copy a work without obtaining the rightholder's permission, unless your intended use of copies qualifies for "fair use," explained in Chapter Five. Because copyright duration is so long, it is generally impractical to analyze whether or not to procure permission to copy a work based solely on the date it was published. Unless the field involves history, literature, archaeology, or similar disciplines concerned with works of antiquity, most materials used for research and projects on campus will be relatively current and well within the duration of copyrights. Rather than trying to meticulously identify if a copyright still applies, it is advisable to pursue obtaining permission or to determine if the need falls under the fair use category.

Public Domain

When copyrights expire, exclusive rights to copy the work cease and the work is said to "merge into the public domain." In other words, the public at large may copy the work freely at will.

There are other works as well that are considered in the public domain. For example, all works published by the United States federal government are in the public domain from the outset.[4] The user should, however, make certain that the work is, in fact, from the federal government before copying it without permission. Many federal agencies contract with private persons or companies to create and publish information. If the federal government has commissioned a work to be created by a private person or company, the individual or company will own the legitimate copyright to the work. (See "Work-for-Hire" in Chapter One.) It is also important to realize that works created by state or local governments are *not* public domain. Regarded as private works, they have bona fide copyrights and must be treated accordingly.

Some works have been donated to the public domain. Authors and creators may invite anyone to copy their work at will. In this case, there must be a conspicuous statement published with the work that expresses a clear intent that the work is available for copying by the public at large. Anything less than a clear statement authorizing public copying makes it precarious to copy the content without permission.

There are many sites on the Internet that host databases of materials, images, photos, and other content that is purported to be in the public domain. Appendix B lists some of those sites. Proceed cautiously when downloading material from the cyber frontier. Host site declaration that its content is in the public domain does not guarantee the fact. You don't want to end up having to use the defense of "innocent infringer" if you are sued over the issue of using copyrighted material you thought was in the public domain.

Works have also found their way into the public domain through failure to comply with earlier copyright formalities. Before March 1, 1989, the creator had to post a copyright notice to enable copyright protection. Congress recently passed a law that made it possible to revive or cure works that had merged in the public domain because of omitted copyright notices.[5] But that law only applies to works published between January 1, 1978, and March 1, 1989, and then only to works where notice was omitted from "only…a relatively small number of copies… distributed to the public." Additionally, the work must have been registered with the Copyright Office within five years after the publication without notice and a reasonable effort must have been made to provide the notice after the omission was discovered. All works published before 1978 without a copyright notice have lost their copyright protection and have entered the public domain.

In summary, unrestricted copying is permitted of all works in the public domain and includes:

- Works whose copyrights have expired;

Proceed cautiously when downloading material from the cyber frontier. Host site declaration that its content is in the public domain does not guarantee the fact.

- Earlier works that entered the public domain because copyright formalities were not observed;
- Works by the federal government;
- Works donated to the public domain by authors or artists.

There is one other source from which you may copy without restriction: any original work that is your own creation. We sometimes forget that our own work is a source of information which will always be free and unfettered for us to reproduce. Sometimes it is easier to create your own work than to obtain permission or analyze the legal copyright status of pre-existing works.

The Erosion of Public Domain and the Tug-of-War Behind Legislation

There are many who believe, with convincing persuasion, that the public domain of free information, literature, music, and art has been eroding steadily since the enactment of the first U.S. copyright statute in 1790. The Constitution calls for laws protecting copyright "for limited times."[6] The original duration of a copyright was 14 years, with an option to renew for an additional 14 years.[7] Due to successive legislation and U.S. participation in international treaties, including the Sonny Bono Copyright Term Extension Act of 1998, the duration of copyright now extends to the life of the author plus 70 years.[8] The magnitude of this term can be illustrated by the example of a child prodigy. Consider a song written and published by a gifted child at 6 years old. If she lives to be 90, the copyright to the song will have extended 160 years before it migrates into the public domain. Is 160 years a limited time? Has the artist been sufficiently compensated for the work in that time?

A grass-roots movement consisting of several organizations is fighting to save the public domain from what is perceived as further erosion. On January 15, 2003, the U.S. Supreme Court issued an opinion in the case of *Eldred vs. Ashcroft*. This case, dismissed by two lower courts, challenged the Sonny Bono law on the basis that it violates the Constitution by exceeding the power of Congress under the

Copyright Clause, and violates the First Amendment of free speech. The public domain advocates claimed the real intention behind the Sonny Bono law was to keep Walt Disney's copyrights on Mickey Mouse and related cartoon figures from expiring shortly after the turn of the century. The U.S. Attorney General's office, defending the law against the challengers, argued that the new law conforms U.S. copyright duration to European copyright duration in the spirit of reciprocity. (Japan, in turn, has also extended its copyright duration to life plus 70 years to be consistent with Europe and the U.S.)

The Supreme Court held that Congress was within its constitutional powers to extend the duration of copyrights. They said that Congress extended the duration for the purpose of "parity" and "harmonization" so that copyright holders in America have the same duration as copyright holders in Europe. The European Union extended duration to life of the author plus 70 years in 1993. Life plus 70 years is still a limited time.[9]

The case highlights the constant tug-of-war between the special interest groups of education, libraries, and public domain users on one hand and the corporate publishers who own most commercially viable copyrights on the other hand. Compromises for both groups in copyright legislation have resulted in dismally complex legislation, which has frustrated the courts trying to enforce the laws. It is far more difficult yet for the rest of the public to interpret and apply these laws in the context of work, recreation, and education.

> *The duration of copyright now extends to the life of the author plus 70 years.*

Notes

1. 17 USC Section 302(a)
2. 17 USC Section 302(c)
3. The table in Appendix A is reprinted with permission from Peter B. Hirtle, Director for Instruction and Learning, Cornell University Library
4. 17 USC Section 105
5. 17 USC Section 405(a)
6. U.S. Const. Art I, section 1, clause 8
7. Copyright Act of 1709, 8 Anne, c 19; Act of May 31, 1790, 1 Stat. 124-5
8. 17 USC Section 302(a)
9. *Eldred vs. Ashcroft,* 537 U.S. ____(2003) (Full citation presently unavailable. See opinion at http://caselaw.lp.findlaw.com/us/0000/01-618.html)

Chapter Three

Copyright Infringement Lawsuits— The Risk of Infringing

No one really knows how pervasive copyright infringement is. But it is probably a safe guess that only a relatively few number of incidents are actually discovered by the copyright holder. Of incidents that are discovered, far fewer wind up in court. In the university community, the issue is more about personal ethics than the consequences of getting caught. Fundamentally, the issue hinges on the degree of individuals' willingness to comply with laws and policies in regard to their own use of others' artistic and intellectual property. On every campus there's a spectrum of ethical perspective and behavior—from callous disregard to pious compliance.

Whatever the motivation for complying or not complying with copyright law, the consequence of losing an infringement lawsuit is worth learning.

The Chain of Liability

As in most civil litigation, the plaintiff tries to join as many defendants as possible in copyright lawsuits. The reason for this is to increase the likelihood of collecting a judgment or settlement. Legal procedure sets up a chain of liability, like tentacles growing outward from ground zero. For example, a copy shop makes copies of a textbook for a professor for use in his class. A teaching assistant delivers the order, pays for the copies and picks up the finished copies. The copy shop's employees take the order and make the copies. The publisher of the textbook discovers the copies and files a lawsuit. Who will be named as defendants?

At ground zero, the professor is directly liable. He instigated the illegal copying, set the process in motion and directly benefited by the result. He is the first target in the infringement lawsuit. Next in line

On every campus there's a spectrum of ethical perspective and behavior—from callous disregard to pious compliance.

of liability are those who are involved in **contributory infringement:**

[O]ne who, with knowledge of the infringing activity, induces, causes or materially contributes to the infringing conduct of another, may be liable as a 'contributory' infringer…Put differently, liability exists if the defendant engages in personal conduct that encourages or assists the infringement.[1]

This means that if someone knows about the infringing activity and acts in a way to incite, assist, or further the infringement, that person is a contributory infringer. "Knowledge of the infringing activity" does not mean that someone knows that a violation of copyright law is occurring. It simply means that a person is aware that copies have been made. Ignorance of the law is no defense. The employees of the copy shop are liable because they knew that the book was copied and they participated in the act. Even the teaching assistant is liable because of his participation. This type of liability is known as "contributory copyright infringement."

The chain of liability goes even farther. People may be liable even if they don't have any knowledge of the infringing activity. This is known as **vicarious infringement:**

The absence of such language in the copyright statute does not preclude the imposition of liability for copyright infringement on certain parties who have not themselves engaged in the infringing activity. For vicarious liability is imposed in virtually all areas of the law, and the concept of contributory infringement is merely a species of the broader problem of identifying the circumstances in which it is just to hold one individual accountable for the actions of another.[2]

Liability in copyright infringement without knowledge of the infringing activity is known as vicarious liability. "Unlike contributory infringement, knowledge is not an element of vicarious liability."[3] A judge explains this further:

In the context of copyright law, vicarious liability extends beyond an employer/employee relationship to cases in which a defendant "has the right and ability to supervise the infringing activity and also has a direct financial interest in such activities."[4]

Thus, the owner of the copy shop and even the university that employed the professor might be liable for copyright infringement if the copyright holder proves that either one had the "right and ability to supervise the infringing activity."

Actual or Statutory Damages

In a copyright infringement lawsuit, the copyright holder must prove that: 1) he owns a valid copyright and 2) constituent elements of the work that are original were infringed.[5] If liability is proved, the copyright holder may elect to recover actual damages or statutory damages. Generally, actual damages include lost profits. The copyright statute recognizes that proving actual damages can often be difficult. In those circumstances, the plaintiff may elect to recover statutory damages. At any time before the court renders a judgement, a copyright holder may elect to recover damages at the statutory rate—from $750 to $30,000 for each incidence of copyright infringement established in trial.[6] If the copyright holder proves that the infringement was committed "willfully," the court has the discretion of requiring the defendent to pay up to $150,000 in addition to statutory damages.[7] On the other hand, if the infringing party proves that "he was not aware and had no reason to believe his or her acts constituted an act of infringement," then the court may reduce statutory damages to an amount not less than $200 per incidence of infringement.[8]

Criminal Offenses

Infringing copyrights for profit or commercial gain can lead to criminal fines and conviction and incarceration in prison. The criminal sanctions in the copyright statute provide that anyone who infringes a copyright "willfully" for the purpose of "commercial advantage or private financial gain" shall be punished by fines or imprisonment, or both.[9] It is also a criminal offense to willfully reproduce or distribute one or more copies of one or more copyrighted works

that have a retail value of $1,000 or more.[10] The offense varies depending on how many copies were made and the value of each copy. The range of punishment is less than a year to five years in prison.[11] For a second conviction of the same offense, the punishment increases to ten years in prison.[12]

Attorneys' Fees

The expense of being involved in litigation begins with attorneys' fees. In infringement cases that involve criminal offenses, the defendant has a right to an attorney and an attorney will be provided if the defendant cannot afford one. In cases that are purely civil in nature, or will result in no criminal liability if the copyright holder prevails, the defendant must hire his own lawyer to represent him. A person may represent himself in a civil trial, but it is ill advised. Among attorneys, a common maxim for people who choose to be their own lawyer is, "They have a fool for a client." An individual is at a tremendous disadvantage without the benefit of a legal professional's expertise in copyright law, legal procedures, and rules of evidence.

The expense of a copyright infringement trial can bankrupt you even if you win the case!

Hiring a defense attorney for a federal copyright infringement trial is expensive. An experienced lawyer in federal practice generally charges $150 or more per hour. The time it takes to prepare for and appear at trial depends on a number of unpredictable factors. It is not unusual for an attorney to bill over a hundred hours before a case even gets to trial. To those unfamiliar with the logistics and costs of litigation, lawyer's fees seem excessive, particularly given the unknown outcome of winning or losing. If you have the time and money to shop for a competent lawyer who charges competitive rates, you will find that the better your defense, the more expensive it is to obtain. Unless you are wealthy, the expense of a copyright infringement trial can bankrupt you even if you win the case!

As if paying your own lawyer isn't sufficient to tax your resources, you may also have to pay for the copyright holder's lawyer if the plaintiff prevails in trial. Recall from Chapter One that the timely registration of copyrights would give a copyright holder both access to the federal courts and a right to recover attorney's fees if she wins an infringement lawsuit.[13]

Mitigating the Risk

So little to gain, so much to lose. We live in a litigious society. Lawsuits are filed every day for such things as serving coffee too hot, or customers slipping on wet spots on the floor of a grocery store. Everyday living entails some risk of being sued. In higher education, the risk of being sued for copyright infringement can be mitigated to tolerable levels. Copyright issues arise on a daily basis, from students, faculty, and administration. The purpose in pointing out what is at stake in losing a copyright lawsuit is to educate people in the consequences and risks of violating copyright law, not to stifle research by suggesting that copies be avoided altogether. Most people involved in higher education will likely be able to legally obtain the material they need to achieve their educational objectives. They only need to learn how.

Notes

1. *A & M Records, Inc. v. Napster, Inc., 239 F.3d 1004,1019 (9th Cir. 2001)*
2. *Sony Corp. v. Universal City Studios, Inc., 464 U.S. 417,435(1984)*
3. M. Nimmer & D. Nimmer, *Nimmer on Copyright*, 3rd ed., Section 12.04[A][1], at 12-70 (1993)
4. *Gershwin Publ'g Corp. v. Columbia Artists Mgmt., Inc., 443 F.2d 1159, 1162 (2d. Cir. 1971)*
5. *Feist Publications, Inc. v. Rural Telephone Service Co., Inc., 499 U.S. 340, 361 (1991)*
6. 17 USC Section 504(c)(1)
7. 17 USC Section 504(c)(2)
8. 17 USC Section 504(c)(2)
9. 17 USC Section 506(a)(1)
10. 17 USC Section 506(a)(2)
11. 18 USC Section 2319(a)
12. 18 USC Section 2319(b)(2)
13. 17 USC Sections 412 and 505

Students participating in typical studies will not need permission to make single copies of materials for personal use in completing class projects, particularly if they will never be published nor uploaded on the Internet. Copying of this nature is clearly within the exception in copyright law known as "fair use." Fair use is covered in Chapter Five.

Permission *is* required for such endeavors as:

- copying small portions of textbooks, journals, and similar media for "course packs."[1]
- copying materials beyond the fair use parameters in anything to be published digitally or in print.
- mass-reproducing or mass-distributing content that is copyright protected that potentially could diminish sales of the same content by commercial publishers and authors who hold the copyrights.

Since most copying or downloading from the Internet that exceeds the limits of fair use will generally fall within the employment duties of faculty, staff, graduate students, or administrative employees, they should know how to obtain permission. Most copy shops are already acquainted with the process for making permission inquiries, since they are regularly involved with producing course packs and related classroom materials from copyright-protected materials. Copy shops typically have a full-time permissions clerk.

Copyright Clearance Center

Obtaining permission can be a time-consuming and frustrating process. But the procedures seem to be improving all the time. The Copyright Clearance Center (CCC) was established in 1978 as a one-stop-shopping place for permission to copy text and print media. Currently, the CCC has accumulated the permission rights to over 1.75 million titles, representing 9,800 publishers.[2] They have a department dedicated to academics. Colleges can request permission to copy materials either as photocopies or as electronic course packs, electronic reserves or distance learning.

The most efficient way to contact the CCC is by visiting their website at **www.copyright.com**. You can also contact them at:

Copyright Clearance Center
222 Rosewood Drive
Danvers, MA 01923

Phone: (978) 750-8400
Email: info@copyright.com

For more contact information, visit the website: **www.copyright.com/About/AboutContactUs.asp**

To use the services of the CCC, you will need to establish an account. For permission to use specific titles, you will need information such as title, author, date or edition of the book, the portion of the work you wish to copy, and the "standard number"—i.e., ISSN, ISBN, or LCCN. All of this information should be available on the copyright notice page. Once you have an account and have supplied the required information, you will usually receive permission immediately. If a request is made by fax, permission typically is given within 24 hours.

Another requirement for permission is the use of a mandatory credit line. The credit line acknowledges the author and cites the original copyright notice. The credit line should be printed in proximity to the pages you have copied and include the identity of the author, © (or the word "copyright"), the year of publication and the phrase, "Reprinted by permission."

If you are an author of a book or related text media, you can join the CCC as a "Rightsholder" and contract with the CCC to grant permission for others to copy your work for a designated royalty fee. In this case, simply visit the CCC website and click on the icon for authors and proceed as instructed.

Permission from the Author or Publisher

Getting permission directly from the author or publisher can be less expensive, but the process presents a greater challenge. Published books rarely provide any information for contacting the author. In many publications, an author's copyrights are assigned to the publishing company. In these cases, permission from the author will be useless because the publisher holds the copyright. Getting permission from a publisher is easier than tracking down an individual author because the name and address of the publisher are usually disclosed on the copyright notice page. With an address, you use a variety of Internet or telephone services to find additional contact information. Most publishers have a "permission desk" or department to assist you.

Sometimes you may discover that the publishing company is no longer listed, and may have gone out of business. Your only hope at this stage is to contact the CCC and see if they have the title, which is why it's a good idea to start with the CCC originally. If the CCC doesn't have the title, your search for permission can entail real gumshoe detective work.

Another possibility for locating the copyright holder is to contact the U.S. Copyright office via the web at: **www.copyright.gov**. You can search the copyright records under the name of the title or author and look at the contact address. Again, if the copyright was assigned to the publisher, the publisher is likely to be the contact listed. Many authors who self-publish a book do not register the copyright. You may find yourself back at square one, trying to locate one individual among hundreds of millions. If all else fails in your endeavor to obtain permission, you are left with the choice of using the work under fair use without permission, or not copying the work at all.

Permission for Photographs or Images

Since photographs are protected by copyright, you should presume that *all* images, whether photographs or not, are protected. Because images and photos by themselves are considered to be entire works, there is far less likelihood that you may use them without permission under the copyright exception of fair use. One of the four factors for determining fair use is what portion of the work will be copied. If an image or photograph is copied, the entire work has been copied. This factor does not automatically disqualify the use of an image from being covered by fair use because there are still three other factors to consider. But it does indicate that the other three factors should weigh more heavily in favor of fair use than in cases where only a small portion of a work is copied. (Refer to Chapter Five.)

Almost everyone is familiar with the popular cartoon, "The Far Side," by Gary Larson. His cartoons were published in newspapers, books, and other print media for many years until he retired in the late '90s. When he discovered that people were uploading his work on the Internet, he posted a very courteous letter to the public at large, requesting that his fans "cease and desist" from posting his cartoons online. Here are portions of his letter:

I'm walking a fine line here.

On the one hand, I confess to finding it quite flattering that fans have created websites displaying and/or distributing my work on the Internet. And on the other, I'm struggling to find the words that convincingly but sensitively persuade these Far Side enthusiasts to "cease and desist" before they have to read these words from some lawyer.

> *Presume that all images, whether photographs or not, are protected.*

…To attempt to be "funny" is a very scary, risk-laden proposition. (Ask any stand-up comic who has ever "bombed" on stage.) But if there was ever an axiom to follow in this business, it would be this: Be honest to yourself and—most important—respect your audience.

So, in a nut shell (probably an unfortunate choice of words for me), I ask only that this respect be returned, and the way for anyone to do that is to please, please refrain from putting The Far Side out on the Internet. These cartoons are my "children" of sorts, and like a parent I'm concerned about where they go at night without telling me. And seeing them at someone's website is like getting the call at 2:00 a.m., that goes, "Uh, Dad, You're not going to like this much, but guess where I am."

I hope my explanation helps you to understand the importance this has for me personally, and why I'm making this request.

Please send my "kids" home. I'll be eternally gratefully,

GL[3]

"Cease and desist" is a common phrase used by lawyers for warning someone to stop infringing their client's rights. Gary Larson's letter may well be the most polite and gracious demand letter in the history of litigation. The point is this: images, such as cartoons, are protected by copyright and, unless your use qualifies under fair use, you need permission to copy, display, or post them on the Internet. Even if you just want to use one as computer wallpaper, get permission first.

Getting permission for photos or images that you wish to copy is nearly impossible. This is because there is seldom any information on the image or photo itself that would lead you to the copyright holder. It is rare to find one displaying a copyright notice. Even then you have only the identity of the copyright holder and face the daunting task of locating that person to solicit permission. So you are better off either conducting a fair use analysis or creating an image or taking a suitable photograph yourself. If something is your own work, you can do with it as you please.

Another approach is to locate images or photos that are offered to be copied for free or for a fee. There are several websites that have large databases of images and photos available for selection. Here is a sampling:

- Fotosearch.com
- Ofoto.com
- Image.altavista.com
- Corbis.com
- ClipArt.com

For simplicity in complying with copyright laws, start with materials that already have permission issues resolved.

Permission to Play Music in Public

Anyone who plays music in public should obtain permission to do so. It is generally easy to find the correct source for procuring permission to play music. Permission licensing is handled by certain licensing agencies. Who should get permission? Anyone playing live or recorded music in public—in any place where a large group of people might be listening. This includes, but is not limited to:

- radio stations, bars, nightclubs, and jukebox operators;[4]
- hotels that play the radio for guests through speakers or headphones;[5]
- restaurants;[6]
- stores;[7]
- telephone intercom systems that play music while callers are on hold;[8]
- public address systems.

Who should get permission? Anyone playing live or recorded music in public—in any place where a large group of people might be listening.

Copyright law only gives the artist or publisher the right to control *public* performances. Private performances are not prohibited. This is what gives people the right to view home videos with family members or a small group of friends, to play a song on the piano, or to listen to music on a tape or CD in the car. But the line between private and public performances is not very clear, making it advisable to err on the side of caution.

The copyrights of music performances are licensed by agencies such as the American Society of Composers, Authors and Publishers (ASCAP) and Broadcast Music, Inc. (BMI). Both agencies actively enforce their members' copyrights. To illustrate both the gray zone between public and private performance, and the zeal with which the licensing agencies protect their market, consider the recent plight of the Girl Scouts. It is reported that ASCAP sent a letter to the Girl Scouts of America, demanding hundreds of dollars in annual royalties for music played and songs sung at club functions, including campfire get-togethers. Someone at ASCAP was heard to complain, "They buy twine and glue for their crafts… they can pay for their music, too." When, in protest, Girl Scouts learned "the Macarena" in silence, it generated enough publicity to assist efforts to enact laws that exempt certain limited public performances.[9]

There are some additional exemptions to the right to publicly perform a work,[10] but they are very limited; even judges sometimes disagree about where they apply.

Applying for a license to perform music in public can be done over the Internet. This type of license is called a "mechanical license," even though it applies only to live performances, because the rules and rates for the license are established by law. Since you are not likely to know in advance which licensing agency manages your selection(s), you may need to contact each of the following:

- American Society of Composers, Authors and Publishers (ASCAP):
    Website: www.ascap.com
    Email: info@ascap.com
    Telephone: (212) 621-6000

- Broadcast Music, Inc. (BMI):
    Website: www.BMI.com
    Email: genlic@bmi.com
    Telephone: (800) 925-8451

- Society of European Stage Authors and Composers (SESAC) :
    Email: license@sesac.com
    Telephone: (800) 826-9996 in Nashville
    　　　　　(212) 586-3450 in New York

There is a separate licensing agency for music sound recordings, which is separate from performance rights. Contact the Harry Fox Agency for a license for sound recording rights.

- Harry Fox Agency:
    www.nmpa.org/hfa.html

These sites will help determine who owns the license to music you want to play in public. Conduct a search of the repertoire for each agency by the title and artist of the songs you wish to play.

The operating dynamics of music licensing agencies are highly complex and exceed the subject of this book. For a more detailed description of these dynamics, refer to the Barry M. Massarsky article posted at:

www.ifla.org/documents/infopol/copyright/massarsk.txt

Notes

1. *Princeton University Press v. Michigan Document Service, Inc., 99F.3d 1381 (6th Cir. 1996) Cert. Den'd 117 S.Ct. 1336 (1997)*
2. www.copyright.com/About/default.asp
3. http://farside.lindesign.se/
4. *Broadcast Music, Inc. vs. Star Amusement, Inc.* (7th Cir.) (http://findlaw.com/7th/934074.html)
5. *Buck vs. Jewell-La Salle Realty Co.,* 283 U.S. 191(1931) (http://findlaw.com/us/283/191.html
6. *Red Cloud Music Co. vs. Schneegarten,* 27 USPQ2d 1319 (CD Cal 1992)
7. *Mole Music vs. Mavar's Supermarket,* 12 USPQ2d 1209 (ND Ohio 1989)
8. *Prophet Music, Inc. vs. Shamla Oil Co.,* 26 USPQ2d 1554 (DC Minn 1993)
9. *Zittrain: Call Off the Copyright War,* Seth Johnson, http://lists.microshaft.org/pipermail/dmca_discuss/2002-November/004056.html]
10. 17 USC Section 110

Chapter Five

The Mystic Doctrine of Fair Use

Fair Use is one of the most unsettled areas of the law. The doctrine has been said to be "so flexible as to virtually defy definition."
—David Nelson, Circuit Judge for the Sixth Circuit, in *Princeton University Press, et al. vs. Michigan Document Services*[1]

Controversial Nature and Purpose

The exclusive rights conferred upon artists, authors, and composers by the copyright laws were never intended to be unlimited. Even the Copyright Clause of the Constitution provides that any laws protecting copyright must be for "limited times" and for the purpose of promoting "the progress of science and the useful arts."[2] A Supreme Court Justice once said that the Fair Use Doctrine "permits courts to avoid rigid application of the copyright statute when, on occasion, it would stifle the very creativity which that law is designed to foster."[3] So there are instances in which copying someone else's work without their permission is "fair" and legal. The problem is that there are no clear legal guidelines that spell out what those instances are.

Fair use was originally created by the courts. In 1978, it was codified by Congress in Title 17, Section 107 of the U.S. Code. The intention was to simply restate the doctrine as it existed, not to revise, limit or expand the concept in any way.[4] Because the courts defined the concept so broadly, and in many cases inconsistently, the confusing nature of the limits of the doctrine survived codification. Since enactment of the statute, the courts still struggle with the fair use analysis.

A recent case which addresses copying materials for classroom projects is a prime example of the controversial nature of fair use. In the first ruling by the Sixth Circuit in *Princeton University Press, et al. vs. Michigan Document Services, Inc.*, by a three-judge panel, it was held that "course packs" containing copies of portions of copyrighted works reproduced without permission constituted fair use. This ruling reversed the lower District Court decision which held that course packs were not fair use and therefore constituted willful copyright infringement. The publishers who lost the appeal filed a motion for rehearing before a full panel of the Circuit Court and the full panel, consisting of thirteen judges (referred to as *en banc*), decided to hear the case. The full Court reversed the three-judge panel opinion and held that course packs were not fair use and, as such, the copy shop infringed the works of the copyright holders, i.e., the publishing companies. That decision was divided by eight to five. Of the five judges supporting fair use, three wrote separate dissents, each expressing a different reason for their conclusion. Thus several judges on the same court could not agree where the limits of fair use begin and end—at least in regard to copying classroom materials.

The Federal Statute: 17 U.S.C. Section 107

The federal statute which codified fair use provides:

Notwithstanding the provisions of sections 106 and 106A, the fair use of a copyrighted work, including such use by reproduction in copies or phonorecords or by any other means specified by that section, for purposes such as criticism, comment, news reporting, teaching (including multiple copies for classroom use), scholarship or research, is not an infringement of copyright. In determining whether the use made of a work in any particular case is a fair use the factors to be considered shall include:

(1) The purpose and character of the use, including whether such use is of a commercial nature or is for nonprofit educational purposes;

(2) The nature of the copyrighted work;

(3) The amount and substantiality of the portion used in relation to the copyrighted work as a whole; and

(4) The effect upon the potential market for or value of the copyrighted work.

The fact that a work is unpublished shall not by itself bar a finding of fair use if such finding is made upon consideration of all the above factors.

According to the limitations of the statute, copying works without permission is permitted for "purposes such as criticism, comment, news reporting, teaching, scholarship or research." For example, copying in the pursuit of journalism or education (both learning and teaching) would qualify at the threshold of the fair use analysis. Then, once the purpose is determined to be appropriate, the four factors should be considered. Contrary to popular belief, educational purpose by itself does not guarantee fair use.

The Four Factors of Fair Use

As written, the four factors of fair use seem confusing. Let's compare how the courts consider each factor.

Section 107(1): The Purpose and Character of the Use

Is the purpose of copying someone's work for commercial gain or nonprofit education? Does it have any other purpose? Is the use of someone's work for the purpose of criticism, comment, news reporting, teaching, scholarship or research? A nonprofit use for the purpose of any of the foregoing will weight this factor in favor of fair use.

Another purpose which leads to a finding of fair use is borrowing from the original product to make a new product. The U.S. Supreme Court has called this a "transformative use," or "transformative work."[5] Many cases have held parodies of original works to be fair use because the humorous comment on or criticism of the original transforms the unauthorized copying into a new work of art. The nature of parody requires borrowing elements from the original in order to mimic or make the criticism of the original. The courts do not determine whether the comedy of parodies is in good taste, only that an attempt at commenting or criticizing the original work be made. The following are parodies that the courts ruled as fair use and not copyright infringement:

- "When Sonny Sniffs Glue," a parody of "When Sonny Gets Blue."[6]
- "I Love Sodom" a Saturday Night Live parody of "I Love New York."[7]

Section 107(2): The Nature of the Copyrighted Work

What is the nature of the original work that is being copied? How creative is it? Is it entirely creative, as in fiction or drama? Or is it non-creative, like alphabetic telephone book listings? The more creative the nature, the more this factor weighs against fair use. The less creative, say, in the case of telephone book listings or lists of statistics, the more the factor weighs in favor of fair use. In an example of contrasting works, the script for the play *Fiddler on the Roof* is far more creative than the newspaper review that critiques the play. Therefore, there is a higher likelihood that copying the newspaper review would be considered fair use than copying the playwright's script.

Section 107(3): The Amount and Substantiality of the Portion Used in Relation to the Copyrighted Work as a Whole

This factor takes into consideration not only the quantity of the work used, but the quality and importance of the portion used.[8] As one legal scholar stated, "the larger the volume (or the greater the importance) of what is taken, the greater the affront to the interests of the copyright owner, and the less likely the taking will qualify as a fair use."[9] Section 107(3) doesn't place any hard limits or boundaries on what is too much or what is too important. Since there are an infinite number of circumstances that may surround a copyright infringement case, particularly due to the nature of the arts in general, it is not practical or realistic to establish hard limits or percentages that define how much "taking" is too much. "There is no bright-line rule to tell us how large of an excerpt renders it unfair as a matter of law, nor how small an excerpt is so small as to be conclusively fair."[10] We can examine specific infringement cases where fair use was raised as a defense and see where the courts have drawn the line. From the following cases, the amounts or importance used weighed *against* fair use:

- 300–400 words (13% of the total original) of Gerald Ford's memoirs weighed against fair use because it was the "heart" of the work or significant "qualitative value." *Harper & Row Publishers, Inc. v. Nation Enterprises*[11]
- 95 pages (30% of total), 45 pages (18% of total), 78 pages (16% of total), 52 pages (8% of total), 77 pages (18% of total) and 17 pages (5% of total), 8000 words in the shortest excerpt in course packs for class weighed against fair use. *Princeton University Press v. Michigan Document Services, Inc.*[12]
- Entire articles making a "small percentage" of the periodical in which they were published weighed against fair use. *American Geophysical Union v. Texaco, Inc.*[13]
- Multiple copies for class with an excerpt of 50% of the original Cake Decorating Book weighed against fair use. *Marcus v. Rowley.*[14]

A relatively recent U.S. Supreme Court case found in favor of fair use even though the use of the original work was substantial. The court distinguished the case as being unique because the product that used substantial portions of the original—a musical parody—was in a separate class than the cases on course packs and text. In *Campbell v. Acuff-Rose Music, Inc.,* the rap group 2 Live Crew released a song that was a parody of the Roy Orbison song, "Oh, Pretty Woman." The original song has lyrics that are essentially romantic and innocent. 2 Live Crew used the same bass line and first verse as the original "Pretty Woman" but altered the lyrics in subsequent

verses to "big hairy woman," then "baldheaded woman," then finally, "two-timin' woman."[15] The court admitted that the level of actual humor generated by the parody was questionable. But judgment of humor has no place in the analysis of fair use. As to amount and substantiality of the portion of the original used, the court explained:

Parody presents a difficult case. Parody's humor, or in any event its comment, necessarily springs from recognizable allusion to its object through distorted imitation. Its art lies in the tension between a known original and its parodic twin. When parody takes aim at a particular original work, the parody must be able to "conjure up" at least enough of that original to make the object of its critical wit recognizable. What makes for this recognition is quotation of the original's most distinctive or memorable features, which the parodist can be sure the audience will know. Once enough has been taken to assure identification, how much more is reasonable will depend, say, on the extent to which the song's overriding purpose and character is to parody the original or, in contrast, the likelihood that the parody may serve as a market substitute for the original. But using some characteristic features cannot be avoided.[16]

We can see how the fair use factors of Section 107 interact with one another. In "Pretty Woman," 2 Live Crew's use of the original song was for the purpose of creating more music or art. Recall that the first factor in Section 107(1) was the purpose and character of the use. Because that factor found that the purpose and character of the "Pretty Woman" parody was "transformative," or for the purpose of creating more music or art, the fact that a substantial portion of the original was used was greatly mitigated. The court was more forgiving of taking a large portion because of the new work created by it.

Section 107(4): The Effect of the Use upon the Potential Market for or Value of the Copyrighted Work

Of the four factors for determining fair use, the fourth factor, effect upon potential market, has been said to be the most important.[17] But the importance of this factor seems to vary by the type of case the courts consider. For example, in the *Campbell* parody case, the first factor determined that the purpose and character of the parody song was indisputably commercial in nature. As this was the nature of the song, 2 Live Crew had the burden of proving that there was no appreciable potential for harming the market for Roy Orbison's song. The Supreme Court concluded that entirely different styles or genres of music have entirely different markets. In other words, the type of person who enjoys Roy Orbison's music is unlikely to enjoy 2 Live Crew's music. Therefore, since 2 Live Crew's parody had demand in a totally different market, no potential harm would result to the market for the original song.[18]

In cases where materials for the classroom were copied from originals, the fourth factor is the most important. In *Princeton University Press,* the court said that, although the use of the copied materials by the faculty and students wasn't commercial in nature, the duplication and selling of the materials by the copy shop was.[19] When the copy endangers the market for the original, this factor weighs against fair use.

Another consideration in this factor in analyzing fair use is "whether unrestricted and widespread conduct of the sort engaged in by the defendant…would result in a substantially adverse impact on the potential market."[20] In other words, finding that that the widespread practice of making similar copies *might* adversely impact the market for the copyrighted work also weighs against fair use.

Because the court has ruled that either actual or potential market impact weighs against fair use, the message to the user is clear: *obtain permission before copying the work.*

Analyzing the Four Factors

The fair use statute gives little guidance on how the four factors should be analyzed. In fact, Section 107 states merely that the four factors should be "considered." The statute goes on to say, "The fact that a work is unpublished shall not itself bar a finding of fair use if such finding is made upon consideration of all the above factors."

The courts have scoured all the legislative history of Section 107 for guidance and made some conclusions about how the four factors interplay. The U. S. Supreme Court writes:

Congress has plainly instructed us that fair use analysis calls for a sensitive balancing of interests. The distinction between "productive" and "unproductive" uses may be helpful in calibrating the balance, but it cannot be wholly determinative. Although copying to promote a scholarly endeavor certainly has a stronger claim to fair use than copying to avoid interrupting a poker game, the question is not simply two-dimensional. For one thing, it is not true that all copyrights are fungible. Some copyrights govern material with broad potential secondary markets. Such material may well have a broader claim to protection because of the greater potential for commercial harm. Copying a news broadcast may have a stronger claim to fair use than copying a motion picture. And, of course, not all uses are fungible. Copying for commercial gain has a much weaker claim to fair use than copying for personal enrichment. But the notion of social "productivity" cannot be a complete answer to this analysis. A teacher who copies to prepare lecture notes is clearly productive. But so is a teacher who copies for the sake of broadening his personal understanding of his specialty. Or a legislator who copies for the sake of broadening her understanding of what her constituents are watching; or a constituent who copies a news program to help make a decision on how to vote.[21]

When the courts analyze fair use, they look at the evidence and apply the facts to each factor. Accordingly, each factor tips either in favor of fair use or against it. After all four factors are considered, a majority of factors leaning toward fair use theoretically resolve the issue in favor of fair use. But this process is not susceptible to any production-line formula. Remember that the U.S. Supreme Court has said that the Fair Use Doctrine "permits courts to avoid rigid application of the copyright statute when, on occasion, it would stifle the very creativity which that law is designed to foster."[22]

Let's consider how facts tip each factor either for or against fair use.

Applying the Facts

❖ Purpose and Character of the Use

The fair use statute expressly provides specific purposes for using someone else's work that may lead to qualifying as fair use. But the courts have found

additional purposes to support fair use, such as the interest of the general public. One court held that copying Sony's screen shots for a PlayStation game by a company for comparative advertising was a proper purpose even though it was clearly commercial in nature. The Ninth Circuit Court of Appeals ruled that even though the purpose of copying the game screen shots was commercial, "such comparative advertising redounds greatly to the purchasing public's benefit with very little corresponding loss to the integrity of Sony's copyrighted material."[23] This is a prime example of balancing interests in fair use analysis. It is not only the respective interests of the copier and copyright holder that are considered.

Regarding analyzing fair use on campus, the purposes stated in the fair use statute—"criticism, comment, news reporting, teaching (including multiple copies for class room use), scholarship or research"[24]—will apply to most copying activities. A common misconception on college campuses is that an educational purpose, by itself, is sufficient to establish fair use and, thus, no permission is required. A correct purpose is only one of four factors that lead to a conclusion that a use is fair. So the facts must be applied to all four factors to reach a conclusion about whether copying or downloading others' materials is truly within the scope of fair use. Generally speaking, any commercial purpose for making copies is not considered fair use. The present exceptions to this are:

> *A common misconception on college campuses is that an educational purpose, by itself, is sufficient to establish fair use and, thus, no permission is required.*

- Copies made for a "transformative" purpose, such as a parody, in which case the copy is necessary for the creation of another artistic work in its own right. Another example might involve using a portion of someone's materials for a teaching aid or model to assist in learning a principle or theory.
- Copies made for some purpose which benefits the general public, as in copying the image of another company's product for comparative advertising.

Any purpose which advances education, teaching, research, or journalism (news reporting, comment or criticism) falls under the purpose of fair use.

However, it is easy to blur the purpose of a copy when it occurs in the context of an academic activity. Take, for example, the production of a class videotape illustrating various seashells of the world. This would be considered a correct purpose to use someone's photos of seashells. But using the theme song to *Sponge Bob* from television cartoons for the video's background sound track may not constitute a correct purpose because it serves only as entertainment, not education. So, the distinction must be made between that which truly furthers education or research and that which merely entertains.

❖ Nature of the Material Copied

This factor requires considering the amount of creativity invested in the original work you want to copy. Works that are artistic or creative in nature are more zealously protected by copyright law than factual, nonfiction data. It is harder to justify copies of highly artistic works—such as poems, plays, fiction, music, and paintings—within the scope of fair use. Conversely, works that provide mere data or factual information weigh more in favor of fair use.

Texaco was sued after making hundreds of copies of journals for which the company had purchased only a few subscriptions. As many as 500 research scientists at Texaco could request the copies. The Second Circuit Court of Appeals decided that the practice of making so many copies from only a few subscriptions exceeded fair use. However, because the articles were mostly factual in nature—i. e., scientific data—the second factor of fair use, regarding the nature of the materials copied, was in favor of fair use.[25] But, because the weight of the other three factors were against fair use, the company was found by the court to have infringed copyright.

Another aspect to consider is whether or not the material to be copied was ever actually published. Under common law, authors possess the right to be the first to publish their works—called the right to "publish first." As a result, unpublished works are regarded as less available for fair use. But what about copying published works that are out of print? Here, the law is nebulous. On one hand, out-of-print works may lean against fair use because they are no longer published. On the other hand, the fourth factor of analysis could tip the balance toward fair use because there is little market, if any, for selling an out-of-print work. If there is no product to sell, an author or publisher could hardly complain about losing profits because of unauthorized copies. Extended, this rationale could possibly apply to works that have never been published; after all, what sales market is there to be affected? Until the issue is finally resolved, it is advisable to obtain permission before copying an unpublished work.

❖ Amount of the Copyrighted Work Used

Section 107(3) does not place a numerical limit on how much is too much for fair use. Copying an entire work may make this factor weigh against fair use, but not rule fair use out conclusively. The less you copy, the more likely you qualify for fair use. Copying what is essentially the "heart" of a work is tantamount to copying the entire work. There will be occasions in the pursuit of higher education where copying the heart of a work, if not the entire work, is unavoidable. For instance, it would be considered using the whole work to copy a photo of an old building in Florence, Italy, to depict ancient Florentine architecture. Or it might be considered as using the heart of a work to copy a graph showing the correlation of the effects of two drugs on the human nervous system for a pharmacy class. In such cases, it is important to remember that if this factor tips largely against fair use, then the other three factors should tip largely in favor of fair use to offset this one's negative value.

Conversely, if only a minute amount is copied, in terms of both quantitative and qualitative aspects, then there is more latitude in the other factors to tip against fair use and still ultimately qualify for it.

Of the four fair use factors, the amount of the copyrighted work used can be the easiest factor manipulated to bring a copy project into acceptable boundaries for fair use. If a work is fictional or otherwise highly creative, as in a drama script, the nature of the work will weigh against fair use copying.

Copying what is essentially the "heart" of a work is tantamount to copying the entire work.

In order to offset the negative value in that factor, the amount of the play to be copied could be reduced from several acts to a single act or even a few lines, depending on the educational objective.

As people get accustomed to balancing the fair use factors, they can design copy projects from the outset with the aim of qualifying for fair use. This is far wiser than proceeding with a copy project, analyzing fair use factors afterward, and then having to deal with the quandary of what to do about the project if the fair use analysis proves negative.

❖ The Commercial Effect

To what extent will a copy project diminish sales of the original product? To what extent will a copy project have a *potential* to diminish sales of the original product? Would you be competing with the author or publisher by using copies of the originals? Are the copies being used as a substitute for the originals? These are the salient inquiries to be made in applying facts to the fair use factor of commercial effect. If using copies replaces, or has the potential to replace, the original product, then this factor tips against fair use. Of the four factors, commercial effect proves the most difficult to analyze.

Focus first on what exactly the copyright owner's market really is. Some copyright owners, or "rightsholders," take the commercial hard line that an original product should be purchased for every situation. But this position ignores the fair use statute outright. There is a limit to a rightsholder's market, but there has been no consensus in court opinions regarding those limits. One court made the distinction between the market for a single scientific article and the market for several scientific articles, applying the following logic: A journal is published to sell a collection of articles, or the content from cover to cover otherwise. A journal is not published to sell a single article. Since journals consisting of a single article are rarely published, it follows that there is very little to no market for single articles.[26] There has to be a bona fide market that is adversely affected to tip this factor against fair use. However, other courts have held that the very existence of the Copyright Clearance Center (see Chapter

Four) has now created a commercial market for copies of single articles. In the opinion of these courts, no use of any complete article can be presumed to be fair.

After identifying the market for the original product, examine to what extent it may be adversely affected by copying the product. We know that a course pack—a collection of selections from textbooks, journals, and other academically published materials—tips the commercial effect factor against fair use *if* the purpose of making the copies is ultimately commercial or to make a profit.[27] The copy shops that produce course packs earn a profit by making copies for their customers, therefore they are not favored to qualify for fair use.

There is a correlation between the first fair use factor (the nature of the use of copies) and the fourth (commercial effect). If the nature of use is commercial, the commercial effect appears to be adversely affected. But if the nature of use is for parody, comment, or criticism, then there is no correlation. In fact, according to the Supreme Court, if the copy is embodied in a transformative work such as a parody, comment, or criticism, then there will be no adverse commercial effect on the market of the original product because the copies serve an entirely different market.[28]

What if course packs were produced by a non-profit college or university? This is a scenario that has not been addressed by the courts at the time of this writing. Since there is no profit motive in the purpose for the copies—a fact that tips the first factor in favor of fair use—there is no correlation with the fourth factor of commercial effect. But the correlation, in and of itself, only aggravates the fourth factor against fair use. It does not conclusively rule out an adverse commercial effect in the author/publisher's market. The fact that profit is removed from the first factor might turn that factor into a vote *for* fair use, which, in the analysis of course packs not copied for profit, could convert the entire four-factor equation in favor of fair use.

Fair Use Exercises

Like learning a musical instrument, the more you practice fair use analysis, the better you get. It is anything but a consistent science, but we can make do with what the laws and the courts leave us. Human nature is such that opposing interests are prone to sway facts and analyses for their own benefit. For instance, a publisher may consider unauthorized copies of an article published in its journal to be a threat against the reprint market that will reduce royalties that the Copyright Clearance Center collects for granting permission to copy the article. A college professor, however, may conclude that the publisher's true market is selling journals composed of several articles, and that reprints or photocopies are an entirely different market that should not concern the publisher. Neither position is conclusively wrong or right. What matters in court is what the judge concludes, not what the parties think. But believing in good faith that a use is fair is a defense against "willfulness." This highlights the need to temper our personal biases in order to determine fair use as objectively as possible.

What Happens When There are Two Factors For, and Two Against, Fair Use?

With four principal factors to consider, sometimes there's a draw. If this happens, the facts must be weighed carefully in order to determine which factor should break the tie. This test should not be conducted rigidly, but with consideration of what is fair to copyright holders and what is reasonable for copy users.

The following exercises, which are all based on genuine campus copyright inquiries, are useful for learning to objectively analyze fair use issues.

Exercise 1
Multiple Emails of an Entire Article for Class

Facts: A professor has a subscription to a scientific journal. He has scanned one entire article for a computer file. The article is 20 pages long. He is considering emailing every student in one of his classes and attaching the file with the article. He has 30 students in his class. They would be instructed to read the article to prepare for a test. Does this constitute fair use?

Applying the factors:

1) **Purpose of the Copies:** Scanning materials and duplicating computer files is equivalent to making copies, even though the process is electronic. The purpose is clearly educational. Is there any profit motive? No.
Application: Facts vote FOR fair use.

2) **Nature of Materials Copied:** Scientific articles are generally considered more factual and analytical. This is more susceptible to constituting fair use than fiction or drama.
Application: Facts vote FOR fair use.

3) **Amount of the Copyrighted Work Used:** It may be only one of several articles in the journal, but it is an entire article. If it is the lead article in the journal, it could be the "heart of the work."
Application: Facts vote AGAINST fair use.

4) **The Commercial Effect:** This is where it gets tough. On one hand, the author or publisher may receive royalties for granting permission for others to make copies of excerpts and entire copies of journal articles. If the professor doesn't pay for permission to duplicate and distribute copies of the article, the publisher loses royalty income. So, the project will affect the commercial market. On the other hand, the publisher's real, target market is selling subscriptions for the entire journal. The professor has already paid for a subscription. Should all the students in class buy a subscription for a year's worth of journals to do an assignment involving only one article? No, that would be unreasonable. How much in permission royalties will the publisher lose? For a majority of titles, the Copyright Clearance Center charges an average royalty based on the following formula:

$$\$0.0075 \times \text{Number of pages} \times \text{Number of copies}$$

Based on the average royalty formula, ($0.0075 x 20 x 30) the publisher will lose $4.50 in permission royalties, a very minimal effect. But what about *potential* effect? What if many classes in colleges all over the country used the article without paying for permission? In this case, it is much too speculative to make any presumption of this nature.
Application: Facts vote FOR fair use.

Conclusion: The email copies would probably qualify for fair use, based on three factors FOR, one factor AGAINST.

Exercise 2
Using Dr. Seuss Expressions and Characters in a Power Point Presentation

Facts: A professor wants to develop an instructional power point presentation on the subject of computer security with the title, "Green Eggs and Spam or The Worm Who Stole Christmas." There are two slides with Dr. Seuss characters and two slides with two to three lines from Dr. Seuss's *Green Eggs and Ham* book. The clear intention is to illustrate computer security tips in four out of 24 slides, using the Dr. Seuss characters and Dr. Seuss lines. For example, "I do not like that spam, Sam I Am, I do not like it at all." In one slide, the Cat in the Hat is holding a plate with the famous green eggs. Instead of the famous ham, there is a drawn likeness of a can of Spam. The presentation is designed for class and continuing education conferences. No commercial application or publication of the presentation is intended.

1) **Purpose of the Copies:** The purpose is educational and no profit motive is involved. Further, the product employing the copyrighted images is transformative in that the presentation is a parody and becomes a copyrighted work in and of itself. Use of the copyrighted images as a parody makes the special rules of parody apply.
Application: Facts vote FOR fair use.

2) **Nature of Materials Copied:** Dr. Seuss characters and lines are highly creative. Works of this nature are the most protected by copyright.
Application: Facts vote AGAINST fair use.

3) **Amount of the Copyrighted Work Used:** The characters and lines actually copied amount to far less than 1% of the whole book. None of the characters or lines are the "heart of the work." As this is a parody, amount of use is highly conservative.
Application: Facts vote FOR fair use.

4) **Commercial Effect:** There is no profit motive in the purpose for using the images and lines. Even if the presentation charged admission for profit, it would not lean against fair use because the use is a parody. Dr. Seuss's products target the children's fiction book market. There is clearly no competition with that market by displaying the presentation in educational settings. Neither is there potential for an adverse effect on Dr. Seuss's market.
Application: Facts vote FOR fair use.

Conclusion: Based on three factors FOR, one factor AGAINST, the use of images in the presentation likely qualifies for fair use.

Exercise 3
Posting a Textbook Online as Classroom Materials

Facts: A college instructor wants to use a textbook she feels is prohibitively expensive. The book is a technical treatise about logarithms in Astrophysics. She decides to upload the book in its entirety on a website that is password protected. Only students enrolled in her class can access the site. Students in her class are instructed to log on and visit the site for reading and assignments.

Purpose of the Copies: The instructor makes one copy by scanning and uploading the book. Students who visit the site make a copy when the textbook is re-created in their personal computer hard drives. The purpose is clearly educational. If the college is a public nonprofit institution there is no commercial nexus.
Application: Facts vote FOR fair use.

Nature of Materials Copied: Since the book is presumably and primarily mathematical equations, very little creativity is present to warrant copyright protection.
Application: Facts vote FOR fair use.

Amount of Copyrighted Work Used: The entire book was copied.
Application: Facts vote AGAINST fair use.

Commercial Effect: There is no profit motive involved for making the copies. But the effect on the market for the book is clearly adverse to the author's/publisher's commercial interests. If the practice were widespread, the cumulative effect could devastate sales for the book. In this example, scanning and uploading a book works easily to substitute for consumers buying the book. The fact pattern is very similar to that of course packs, except that in this scenario the entire book is being duplicated in multiple copies. In this type of case, Commercial Effect is the weightiest of the four factors.
Application: Facts vote AGAINST fair use.

Conclusion: Two factors are FOR fair use. Two factors are AGAINST it. The importance of Commercial Effect breaks the tie. This does not qualify as fair use.

Exercise 4
Student Copies Articles in the Library for Term Paper Research

Facts: A student is doing research for a midterm paper on literature written by Japanese internment camp prisoners during World War II and needs information from nine recent articles in literary journals and periodicals. Assume the articles include mostly large excerpts of poetry and short story fiction. She doesn't like working in the library, so she intends to copy the entirety of each article on the library copy machine and write the paper in her dorm room.

Purpose of the Copies: Clearly educational and nonprofit.
Application: Facts vote FOR fair use.

Nature of Materials Copied: The content of the articles is fictional or dramatic. Copyright law seeks a higher degree of protection the more creative the copyrighted work is.
Application: Facts vote AGAINST fair use.

Amount of Copyrighted Work Used: The articles are copied in their entirety. Even though the articles themselves make up a small percentage of the journals in which they were published, they are separate complete works.
Application: Facts vote AGAINST fair use.

Commercial Effect: Is there any market for single articles published separately from journals? Is it reasonable to require the student to buy the journals containing the articles she wants to use? Her use of the copies is nonprofit. The library doesn't profit from the copy machines she used to copy the articles. Are the articles any substitute for textbooks or materials that are sold in bookstores? Possibly an anthology of articles might be assigned as a class textbook. More likely, the midterm assignment covers only a chapter or section of the class syllabus. There is no real competition within the same market in which the author or publisher sells journals. Thus, there is little or no competition, nor is there likelihood of potential competition.
Application: Facts vote FOR fair use.

Conclusion: Two factors FOR, two factors AGAINST—another tie between the factors. In circumstances like these, a rule of reason should be applied. If students were required to pay for permission royalties just because they are studying literature as opposed to accounting or quantitative analysis, then limiting fair use in favor of authors' and publishers' monetary interests would influence the popularity of subjects in higher education. Students inclined to study literature, drama, or music might choose another field just because it accommodates a limited education budget. Copyright dynamics most likely would favor single copies of entire articles for a single class assignment being considered fair use.

Classroom Guidelines

"The greatest defect of legislative history is its illegitimacy. We are governed by laws, not the intentions of legislators."
—U.S. Supreme Court Justice Scalia in *Conroy v. Aniskoff, Jr.*[29]

"The use of legislative history is the equivalent of entering a crowded cocktail party and looking over the heads of the guests for one's friends."
—Judge Harold Levanthal[30]

There are guidelines for classroom materials used widely on campuses across the country, commonly referred to as "Classroom Guidelines." The full, cumbersome title is, "Agreement on Guidelines for Classroom Copying in Not-for-Profit Educational Institutions with Respect to Books and Periodicals." The Classroom Guidelines were drafted by special interest groups and made a part of committee reports to the federal legislature that enacted revisions to the Copyright Act.[31] Although the Classroom Guidelines were endorsed by the House Report as, "a reasonable interpretation of the *minimum* standards of fair use," they were never enacted as a part of the fair use statute (17 U.S. Section 107)(emphasis supplied). Thus, the Classroom Guidelines have no legal effect whatsoever.[32] Of the special interest groups which reported to the legislative committee, two refused to participate because they considered the proposed guidelines as "too restrictive with respect to classroom situations at the university and graduate level."[33] The two abstaining groups were the American Association of University Professors and the Association of American Law Schools.

Many universities and colleges follow the Classroom Guidelines as though they were federal law. It is reasonable to presume that faculty and administrators who have adopted the guidelines believe, erroneously, that the guidelines *are* federal law. The irony in this is that these institutions of higher education are following legally unsanctioned guidelines that were rejected by their own lobbying groups.

It is easy to see why the guidelines fail in the context of higher education. (See Appendix C for reference to the guidelines.) The limits are too rigid and impractical. "Brevity" limitations are particularly problematic, when only 250 words of a poem can be copied for class, and only complete works of less than 2500 words of prose are allowed. If you want to copy an excerpt, you can only copy 1000 words or less, "or 10% of the work, which ever is less, but in any event a minimum of 500 words." Professors will argue that it is difficult to learn anything meaningful in literature with only 2500 words from Hemmingway, for example. It is apparent that the Classroom Guidelines were framed primarily by groups operating on behalf of copyright holders.

The Classroom Guidelines outline the most conservative and least contentious ground of fair use. However, they are considerably biased in favor of commercial interests that benefit from selling copyrighted materials to the educational market. Because they promote the path of least liability, the guidelines may be a starting point in the fair use analysis, but there is no legitimate legal reason for them to dictate fair use policy in higher education.

Fair Use Analysis Choices

There are options for determining whether a copy project qualifies as fair use. You can use the method suggested in this chapter. You can be most conservative and adopt the Classroom Guidelines. You can dispense with fair use analysis entirely and choose to pay for permission on every copy project. But none of these options guarantees immunity from the possibility of a lawsuit in a litigious society. Many copyright infringement claims come from authors or artists who have no interest in protecting their royalty market. Sometimes, copyright laws are used to control or prevent further publication of works. At times, an author or artist wants no further exposure of their work to the public. Perhaps they discovered or feel their paper was poorly written or based on flawed research, or for some other reason are embarrassed by their work. Or perhaps they highly object to criticism or close scrutiny of their work by others. There are many unrelated reasons for bringing a copyright infringement claim against someone. There is no way to be thoroughly insulated from these claims. However, if you practice fair use judiciously, you can be in a good position to win a lawsuit or defeat an infringement claim.

Institutions can establish their own guidelines to streamline the process of determining fair use, or guidelines already established by others can be used. In Chapter Eight, there is more information about developing customized guidelines. Some fair use-related guidelines available as good resources are located at the following websites:

- www.utsystem.edu/ogc/intellectualproperty/copypol2.htm#course
- http://copyright.iupui.edu/checklist.htm
- www.cetus.org/fair6.html
- www.library.yale.edu/%7Eokerson/georgia.html
- http://ccat.sas.upenn.edu/jod/trln.html

Fair use has been a neglected tool for educational copying for too long. Granted, it is a cumbersome concept to use; it is interpreted by a murky nebula of conflicting legal precedent; it is difficult to apply and difficult to teach others to apply. On the other hand, fair use is the *only* procedure we have for using copyright-protected materials without permission in the pursuit of education. Educators and students need to learn correctly how to use the four factors of fair use in order to make justifiable reproductions of educational materials without the

> *Fair use is the only procedure we have for using copyright-protected materials without permission in the pursuit of education.*

expense and time required to obtain permission when it isn't necessary. In the present world, where information from every corner of the globe is tapped through personal computers, fair use is the legally acceptable path to better education through information retrieval and dissemination.

NOTES

1. Citation: 99 F.3rd 1381 (6th Cir 1996) (*en banc*). Cert. Den'd. 117 S.Ct. 1336 (1997). Opinion also available online at: fairuse.stanford.edu/mds/110896cofadec.html
2. U.S. Constitution, Article I, Section 8
3. *Campbell v. Acuff-Rose Music, Inc.,* 114 S. Ct. 1164, 1170 (1994)
4. *Nimmer on Copyright,* Section 13.05 (1978) citing H. Rep. p. 66
5. *Campbell v. Acuff-Rose Music, Inc.,* 114 S. Ct. 1164 (1994) (http://laws.findlaw.com/us/000/u10426.html)
6. *Fisher v. Dees,* 794 F2d 432 (CA9 1986)
7. *Elsmere Music, Inc. v. National Broadcasting Co.,* 482 F. Supp. 741(SDNY), aff'd, 623 F.3d 252(CA2 1980)
8. *Campbell v. Acuff-Rose Music, Inc.,* 114 S. Ct. 1164 (1994) (http://laws.findlaw.com/us/000/u10426.html)
9. Pierre N. Leval, *Toward a Fair Use Standard,* 103 Harv. L. Rev. 1105, 1122 (1990)
10. Judge Ryan's dissent in *Princeton University Press v. Michigan Document Services, Inc.,* 99 F.3d 1831 (6th Cir. 1996)
11. 471 U.S. 539 (1985)
12. 99 F. 3d 1381 (6th Cir. 1996)
13. 60 F. 3d 913 (2d Cir. 1994)
14. 695 F.2d 1171 (9th Cir. 1983)
15. See www.benedict.com/audio/crew/crew.asp for specific details and commentary
16. *Campbell v. Acuff-Rose Music, Inc.,* 114 S. Ct. 1164 (1994)
17. *Princeton University Press v. Michigan Document Services, Inc.,* 99 F. 3d 1381 (6th Cir. 1996)
18. *Campbell v. Acuff-Rose Music, Inc.,* 114 S. Ct. 1164 (1994)
19. *Princeton University Press v. Michigan Document Services, Inc.,* 99 F. 3d 1381 (6th Cir. 1996)
20. M. Nimmer & D. Nimmer, *Nimmer on Copyright,* 3rd ed., Section 13.05[A] [4], at 13-102.61 (1993)
21. *Sony Corp. v. Universal City Studios, Inc.,* 464 U. S. 417 (1984), at footnote 40
22. *Campbell v. Acuff-Rose Music, Inc.,* 114 S. Ct. 1164, 1170 (1994)
23. *Sony v. Bleem,* Case No. 99-17137 (9th Cir. 2000). Online: laws.findlaw.com/9th/9917137v2.html
24. 17 USC Section 107
25. *American Geophysical Union v. Texaco, Inc.,* 60 F.3d 926 (2d Cir. 1994). Online: www.laws.findlaw.com/2nd/929341.html
26. *American Geophysical Union v. Texaco, Inc.,* 60 F.3d 926 (2d Cir. 1994)
27. *Princeton University Press v. Michigan Document Services, Inc.,* 99 F. 3d 1381 (6th Cir. 1996)
28. *Campbell v. Acuff-Rose Music, Inc.,* 114 S. Ct. 1164, 1170 (1994)
29. From U. S. Supreme Court Justice Scalia in his concurring opinion in *Conroy v. Aniskoff, Jr.,* 507 U. S. 511, 519 (1993)
30. Judge Harold Levanthal's observation quoted in Justice Scalia's concurring opinion, footnote 29, above
31. *Princeton University Press v. Michigan Document Services, Inc.,* 99 F. 3rd 1381(6th Cir. 1996) (Ryan, J. dissenting)
32. See Footnote 31, above
33. House Report, p. 72

Chapter Six

Copyright Law and the Internet

Part of the inhumanity of the computer is that, once it is competently programmed and working smoothly, it is completely honest.
—Isaac Asimov

The Internet has developed much faster than the laws that govern it. Much like the days of the old Wild West, people have found themselves in places where there are no laws to obey or lawmen to enforce them. However, as civilization continues to pour into this new frontier, some laws have been established and the justice system is beginning to enforce them.

Whose Laws, Whose Courts Apply?

In order to enforce civil laws by filing a lawsuit, the court must have jurisdiction over the person who is accused of violating a law. A court acquires jurisdiction over a person when that person makes minimum contact in the state where the court is located. The question of 'minimum contact' becomes complicated within cyberspace. What contact does a person have who created a website in New York that violates the copyrights of a man in Alaska? Is there any contact? Would the Alaskan have to go to New York to file his lawsuit in federal court against the New York man? Cases are starting to define 'minimum contact' in Internet litigation.

Copyright laws apply to the Internet in the same way as they do to the library.

In one case, a website company posted a site with an address of "papalvisit1999.com." The site contained general information about the Pope's visit in 1999. The site also contained advertising of adult sites offering memberships and adult products for sale. It was an apparent bait-and-switch scheme to lure business to the adult sites. The website company was sued in a Missouri federal court by the Archdiocese, which claimed that the website company was infringing its trademark, "papal visit 1999." The court decided that the website company made sufficient minimum contact by operating a website soliciting the business of citizens all over the world, including the United States and Missouri. Further contact was made when several members of the Catholic Church in Missouri complained to the Archdiocese about the papal visit website.[1]

Whether or not website operators make minimum contact in a state other than their own depends partly on the website in controversy. The mere operation of a website—even though available to people in the state where the lawsuit is filed—which only solicits participation or sales, is not sufficient minimum contact for a court to have jurisdiction over the website operator.[2] There has to be some "deliberate action" that is "purposefully directed" in the state for courts in that state to have jurisdiction over the website operator.[3]

In an unpublished decision, the Ninth Circuit Court recently decided that a Washington court had jurisdiction over a website operator who was accused of specifically defaming health care providers in the state with a rating service. The court said the website operator made sufficient minimum contact by posting a rating service that:

purposely interjected itself into the Washington state home health care market through its intentional act of offering ratings of Washington medical service providers. This act was expressly aimed at plaintiff's forum state, since defendant was well aware that its ratings of Washington home health care providers would be of value primarily to Washington consumers.[4]

In determining minimum contact, the approach by the courts, over all, seems to hinge on the "effect" that a website or email has on the aggrieved party or residents in the state where the court is located.

Once a court has established its jurisdiction over the issues and the parties, it can move on to issue a ruling that will be binding on the parties. One of the early published court decisions addressing copyright law as it applies to Internet sites involved the use of photo images on one website that originated on the website of another party.

Downloading and uploading images is so easy over the Internet that copyright issues may not occur to someone using the material. A common misconception among Internet users is that any image found on the "Net" is free to download or copy. In truth, copyright laws apply to the Internet in the same way as they do to the library. Every download of an image or text is equivalent to photocopying a page from a library book.

Uploading Visual Images: Thumbnail Images

Making copies of a photo or another Internet image by saving it to a file on a hard drive is generally considered an infringement of copyright, unless it qualifies as fair use or the image is in the public domain. There is case law now that establishes that "thumbnail" images—images reduced in size in small windows—may be uploaded under fair use. An operator of a search engine was sued for copyright infringement when thumbnail images from another site were copied and posted in the "visual search engine site." When site visitors would click on a thumbnail image, two additional windows would appear: one showing a full-size version of the image and the other showing the full web page where the thumbnail image originated. The court conducted a fair use analysis and found that the most important of the four factors was the first: purpose of the use. The court held that the copy on the search engine was "transformative" in nature; the use of the image in the search engine was different than the way the image was used in the originating site. The originating site used the image for illustrative purposes while the search engine site used it for improving access to images on the Internet.[5]

Making copies of a photo or another Internet image by saving it to a file on a hard drive is generally considered an infringement of copyright, unless it qualifies as fair use or the image is in the public domain.

The ruling would likely have been different had full-sized photos been copied and posted without permission. Full-sized photos have sharper resolution and may be attractive for purchase, thereby serving the economical purposes of the photographer. Low quality thumbnails can be used merely as icons. Thus, there is a different function between full-sized and thumbnail photos. Because the website that copied the photos as thumbnails created essentially a new and useful product, the court ruled that it was fair use and didn't require permission.

Copying "FAQs" from a Website

In order to win a copyright infringement lawsuit you must prove that you owned the copyright to the original work and that the person you are suing copied constituent elements of your work without your permission. Unauthorized copying can be proven by showing the accused infringer had access to the original work and that the copy is substantially similar to the original work.

In a case from Wisconsin, a tanning salon business called "Mist-On Systems" sued a competing tanning salon business called "European Tan Spa" for copying the Frequently Asked Questions (FAQ) portion of a website Mist-On Systems used to promote their business. The court studied the FAQ from Mist-On System's site and the FAQ from European Tan Spa's site. There was no dispute that European Tan Spa had access to Mist-On System's FAQ because the original was posted on the Internet. The only question then was how similar European Tan Spa's FAQ was to Mist-On System's FAQ. The court recognized that ideas and facts by themselves are not protected by copyright. That doesn't mean that the underlying expression of those facts and ideas can't be protected. But in this case, though there were some similarities between the FAQs, there was not enough to prove copying. For example, Mist-On System's FAQ had 19 questions, while European Tan Spa's had 16. Several questions on European Tan Spa's FAQ were not listed on Mist-On System's FAQ. The court decided in favor of European Tan Spa, saying:

A business cannot copyright a Frequently Asked Question page as such or copyright words or phrases commonly used to assemble any given Frequently Asked Questions page. The format of a Frequently Asked Questions page (a list of questions beginning with common words) are stereotypical. Some additional similarity beyond generic formatting is necessary to establish infringement.[6]

Deep Linking

"Deep Linking" refers to the practice of posting an icon on a web page that, when clicked on, will take the visitor to an inner page of another independent site. There has been much controversy with the practice because it creates a shortcut into a website, thereby passing up advertising banners often found on the home page. Website hosts whose sites have been deep linked lose advertising revenue when visitors access their site through a deep link.

Deep linking, in and of itself, is not an infringement of the materials on the site that has been linked.

"Ticketmaster" is a company that sells tickets for various entertainment events online over the Internet. "Tickets.com" also sells tickets to events online. Tickets.com deep linked into Ticketmaster's website with a message that, although they didn't sell tickets to a particular event, the link icon would take visitors to Ticketmaster's site, where they could purchase the tickets. Ticketmaster objected to this and sued Tickets.com under several legal theories, including copyright infringement. The court decided that deep linking is not copyright infringement because there is no copying taking place. The court said, "This is analogous to using a library's card index to get reference to particular items, albeit faster and more efficiently."[7] The court did not dismiss the claim, however, that deep linking is "tortuous interference" by depriving Ticketmaster of advertising income as a result of visitors by-passing the home page. It is predicted that legislation may be introduced that prohibits deep linking a site with advertisement banners on its home page.

Digital Millennium Copyright Act

The Digital Millenium Copyright Act (DMCA) was enacted in 1998 to address the new digital technology. The DMCA implemented sweeping measures

in an attempt to update the law as it pertains to the Internet and new digital technology. The scope and complexity of the DMCA exceeds the subject of this book, but there are some features that impact higher education generally. Title I[8] helps copyright holders protect their work by prohibiting people from circumventing controls created to limit access to or copying of the work. There are CDs that employ a technology to make it impossible to copy them. If someone figures out how to disable the control so they could make copies anyway, they have circumvented a "technological protection measure" and have violated the DMCA. It is also illegal to sell devices that circumvent technological protection measures. There are certain exceptions to anti-circumvention regulations. Non-profit libraries, archives, and educational institutions may circumvent technological protection measures, "solely for the purpose of making a good faith determination as to whether they wish to obtain authorized access to the work."[9]

Title II[10] limits potential monetary damages in a copyright infringement lawsuit in case "Online Service Providers" (OSPs) get sued. OSPs could be vicariously liable for copyright infringement if a subscriber to the online service makes unauthorized copies using the service. The reason is because the OSP provides the means by which copyright infringement takes place. The DMCA limits this liability. Most colleges have computer networks and operate as an OSP, so they can take advantage of this limitation of liability. There are certain requirements that must be satisfied to qualify for this, which include:

- Registering a designated agent with the U.S. Copyright Office to receive and address copyright infringement claims arising from materials that are posted on the school web page and identifying the agent by name and contact information on the web page;

- Posting a notice of copyright policy warning users the service may be terminated for repeat infringement of copyright-protected work;

- Providing "all users of (their) system or network informational materials that accurately describe, and promote compliance with, the laws of the United States relating to copyright."[11]

The DMCA sets up a copyright infringement claim processing procedure that requires any claims relating to materials on a college OSP's website to be submitted to the college's designated agent and contain mandatory information about the claim.[12] Once the designated agent is satisfied that a claim meets the statutory requirements, the owner of the page must be notified, and either a voluntary removal of the materials must be obtained or access disabled. If the college determines later that the materials are not infringing or that they qualify for fair use, they can be restored. The agent must then send a "counter-notice" to the person or agent that submitted the claim, providing the following information:

- The identity of the page owner by physical or digital signature;

- Description of the material that was taken down;

- The page owner's contention that he has a good faith belief that the material was not an infringement and that it was removed by mistake or that it was removed after being erroneously identified;

- The page owner's contact information and that he or she consents to jurisdiction of the federal courts; and that

- The page owner will accept service of the lawsuit citation.[13]

The college will not be liable to the page owner for removing access to the page as long as certain procedures are followed. Access must be restored 10 to 14 business days after the counter-notice is sent to the complaining party, unless the complaining party files an action for a court order preventing reposting of the page.[14]

For more information on the DMCA, see the following websites:

- http://www.ala.org/washoff/dmguide.html
- http://www.educause.edu/issues/dmca.html
- http://arl.cni.org/info/frn/copy/dmca.html
- http://www.eff.org/IP/DMCA/
- http://www.tuxers.net/dmca/

Common Internet Copyright Issues on Campus

"The beginning of knowledge is the discovery of something we do not understand."
—Frank Herbert

As technology has opened up the Internet to people and such abilities as MP3 compression and Peer-to-Peer networking ("P2P") have become common, user knowledge and appreciation of copyright laws appears abysmally nonexistent. There is an alarming popular trend of copying CD music, videos, DVDs, games, and entire movies through the use of personal computers using P2P, MP3, and related technology.

The entertainment industry claims that…the industry will ultimately have to adopt an aggressively litigious position in order to survive, unless the problem is resolved unilaterally by colleges and universities.

Very little, if any, of this activity can be attributed to legitimate educational purposes. Because copies are being made simply for entertainment and without authorization, the purpose doesn't come close to qualifying as fair use. It is flagrant copyright infringement that incurs significant legal liability, not only for those who copy these materials, but for the university that hosts the Internet service that made it possible. To compound the problem, students set up file-swapping sites so that others can download the material.

The entertainment industry claims that billions of dollars are lost and the industry will ultimately have to adopt an aggressively litigious position in order to survive, unless the problem is resolved unilaterally by colleges and universities. Not only do the Goliaths of the entertainment industry have the war chest to hire legions of lawyers to fight this trend, they have the technology to trace every website offering unauthorized files straight to its source: the PC address itself. Though the industry has the means and the justification for launching all-out war in the courts to resolve the problem, their initial strategy is to appeal to the administration and leaders of colleges and universities to self-police their campus Internet networks to curb the practice. Several representatives of the recording and motion picture associations recently sent a letter to 2,300 universities and colleges which presents their plight as follows:

In the past few years, Peer to Peer (P2P) network use has dramatically grown. P2P technology is not only exciting – it may fundamentally change the way digital works are legitimately distributed. However, student trafficking in music, movies, software, video games and other copyrighted materials without authorization on P2P networks not only raises issues of copyright infringement, it is an invitation to invasions of student privacy, viruses and numerous potential security threats to the university's network. A number of forward-looking educational institutions have led the way and have adopted informational and corrective policies aimed at preventing such infringing activity. We applaud these initiatives and would like to support this movement by working with colleges and universities to help establish Codes of Conduct and other procedures to stop theft of creative content.

Copyright Infringement is theft.

The students and other users of your school's network who upload and download infringing copyrighted works without permission of the owners are violating Federal copyright law. "Theft" is a harsh word, but that it is, pure and simple. As Deputy Assistant Attorney General John Malcolm recently stated, "Stealing is stealing is stealing, whether it's done with slight of hand by sticking something in a pocket or it's done with the click of a mouse." It is no different from walking into the campus bookstore and in a clandestine manner walking out with a textbook book without paying for it.

Sheldon E. Steinbach, General Counsel of American Council on Education, said of such illegal file "sharing" activities:

Why is this issue important to higher education institutions? First, educational institutions are in the business of forming student's minds. A fundamental part of this formation is the teaching about ethics, personal responsibility, and respect for the rule of law. Colleges and universities should not be in the business of condoning or promoting unlawful activities.

Additional education about the law with regard to uploading and downloading movies, music, software, games, etc., is essential. Students must know that if they pirate copyrighted works they are subject to legal liability. A number of colleges and universities have already taken positive steps by putting in place codes of online conduct.[15]

Between the lines of this letter is a whispered threat. A reasonable term of peace is for colleges to educate students and others who have access to the campus computer network of the salient provisions of copyright law, which prohibit copying and file swapping of copyright-protected materials that are outside the scope of fair use without permission. Colleges and universities should also review their computer user policies to be sure there is a clear restriction against these activities.

"Copyright infringement is theft." When movies, songs and software are copied without permission, the statement is not mere rhetoric. It can be considered a crime and can be punishable by prison time. The No Electronic Theft Act (NET Act), enacted in 1997, makes willfully sharing copies of copyright-protected products, such as music, movies, or software, a federal crime if the value of the original exceeds $1000 or the person sharing the copy expects to receive files in return. If successfully prosecuted, the person sharing the copies faces one year in prison. If the value of the copied product exceeds $2500, the punishment is up to five years in prison.[16]

On April 3, 2003, the Recording Industry Association of American (RIAA) filed copyright infringement suits against two students at Rensselaer Polytechnic Institute, a student at Princeton and a student at Michigan Technological University. RIAA president, Cary Sherman, declares:

This is a particularly flagrant way to illegally distribute millions of copyrighted works over the Internet. The people who run these 'Napster' networks know full well what they are doing: operating a sophisticated network designed to enable widespread music thievery.[17]

It appears the sheriff's posse is on the trail of student P2P outlaws.

The Internet frontier may never be fully tamed. But it will become more regulated by copyright and other laws in the coming years. As the society grows more reliant on the Internet as an educational, occupational, and recreational tool, it makes good sense to learn to play by the rules.

Notes

1. *Archdiocese of St. Louis v. Internet Entertainment Group, Inc.*, Case No. 4:99CV27SNL, 1999 U. S. Dist. Lexis 1508F (E.D. Mo., Feb. 12, 1999)
2. *American Homecare Federation, Inc. v. Paragon Scientific Corporation*, Case No. CV-893 U.S. Dist. Lexis 17962 (D. Conn., October 26, 1998)
3. *Millennium Enterprises, Inc. v. Millennium Music*, Civ. No. 98-1055-AA (D. Or. Jan., 1999)
4. *Northwest Healthcare Alliance v. Healthgrades.com*, 2002 WL 31246123 (9th Cir. WA)
5. *Leslie Kelly v. Arriba Soft Corp.*, 77 F. Supp. 2d 1116 (C.D. Cal., Dec. 15, 1999)
6. *Mist-On Systems, Inc. v. Gilley's European Tan Spa*, Civ. 02-C-0038-C (W.D. Wis., May 2, 2002)
7. *Ticketmaster Corp. v. Tickets.com, Inc.*, 2000 U.S. Dist. Lexis 4553 (C.D. Ca., March 27, 2000)
8. 17 USC Section 1201
9. See footnote 8, above
10. 17 USC Section 512
11. 17 USC Section 512(e)
12. 17 USC Section 512(c)(2)
13. 17 USC Section 512(g)(3)
14. 17 USC Section 512(g)(1)
15. *Colleges Could Face Lawsuits Over File Sharing*, Katherine S. Mangan, chronicle.com, October 14, 2002
    See http://chronicle.com/free/2002/10/2002101401t.htm
16. *Congress targets campus P2P piracy*, by Declan McCullagh, News.Com (February 26, 2003)
17. Bill Holland, Washington DC, as reported in Billboard.com, April 4, 2003
    www.billboard.com/bb/daily/article_display.jsp?vnu_content_id=1858071

Chapter Seven

Copyright and Distance Education

Technology is a way of organizing the universe so that man doesn't have to experience it.
—Max Frisch

Distance education, or "distance learning," involves teaching outside the traditional classroom environment. Beginning nearly a century ago as "correspondence education," it provided an education for people who could not physically attend schools or colleges.[1] From homework and exams mailed through the postal service, the process has evolved through the use of radio, television, and, presently, the Internet via email and websites. New technology has improved both the quantity and quality of efforts to educate outside the classroom. Distance education will play an increasing role in education for students both inside and outside the college campus.

> *The dynamics of distance education present additional challenges in complying with copyright law, because the the vast majority of course content used in education is copyrighted.*

The dynamics of distance education present additional challenges in complying with copyright law, because the vast majority of course content used in education, whether taught at a distance or in the classroom, is copyrighted. Distance education typically involves the performance or display of works. Posting materials on a website requires making a copy of original materials onto the hard drive of the host computer. Regardless of the technology or equipment used, transmitting any images or sounds from one place to another will generally involve making a copy of original materials. In the classroom, copies made, displayed, or performed under fair use are restricted to the class participants and the purpose for which the copies are made. In classes conducted over the Internet, educational materials may be uploaded, downloaded, and transmitted all over the world— with little or no control over the original purpose of the copied materials. This presents a significant threat to the rights of copyright holders. In many instances it weighs the fair use analysis *against* copies being fair use.

Before 2002, the copyright law did not sufficiently regulate the new technology as it was applied in distance education. But, on November 3, 2002, the "Technology, Education and Copyright Harmonization Act," or "TEACH Act" was signed into law. The intention was to balance the rights of copyright holders with the needs of educators and librarians to use copyright-protected materials in distance education. Now, what can and cannot be copied, shown, or displayed and used in distance education has been expanded, taking the digital age into consideration. However, similar to the Digital Millennium Copyright Act, there are several stringent requirements that must be satisfied before a college or university can qualify under the TEACH Act and be accommodated by the new law.

What the TEACH Act Permits

Section 110(2) of the Copyright Act is repealed. The old section addressed closed-circuit TV education and required a face-to-face classroom environment and only permitted limited types of works to be displayed. The new section has expanded on the use of copies and has removed limits on where educational materials can be displayed. Generally, the TEACH Act now permits the following:

- In a face-to-face classroom environment, you may display or present any materials that relate to the class curriculum, no matter how they are shown. This includes audiovisual and dramatic works like movies, operas, muscials, or music videos.[2]

When class materials are posted online or transmitted over distance, the following guidelines apply:[3]

- Only "reasonable and limited portions" or clips of audiovisual or dramatic materials may be displayed.

- Entire performances of *nondramatic* literary works may be shown or displayed. Examples include reading poetry or short stories.

- Entire performances of *nondramatic* musical works may be shown or displayed. This includes any music other than opera, music videos, or musicals.

- Any still image may be used in its entirety, or portions of displays that compare to displays used in face-to-face classroom environments.

- Students receiving displays or performances of works are no longer restricted to the classroom. They may be situated at any location.

- Any works in an analog format that are not available in a digital format may be digitized.[4]

- Not only can distance education transmissions be recorded and retained as provided by the old law, students can have access to the recorded transmissions for a brief period of time. Copies and storage incidental or necessary in digital transmission are also permitted.

There are many exceptions, limitations, and conditions that must be satisfied before universities may implement these new procedures in their distance education programs. Universities that operate for profit or are unaccredited cannot apply the TEACH Act, because they are specifically excluded. Qualified participants that use distance education in compliance with the TEACH Act are protected from liability from infringement claims against any transitory copies of works made in the process of digital transmissions.

Exceptions, Limitations, and Conditions

Typical of any legislation which survives opposition and conflict by groups of radically different interests, the TEACH Act's benefits to educators come with a price tag. Many universities and colleges are excluded from applying the new procedures. Those that qualify must observe many limitations and satisfy many conditions as a prerequisite to using the new procedures. The salient exceptions, limitations, and conditions follow:

- The new procedures may only be used by a "government body or an accredited nonprofit educational institution."[5]

- The university or college must "institute policies regarding copyright." Although somewhat nebulous, scholars believe this means that a university or college must establish policies requiring compliance with the TEACH Act when using the new procedures for distance education.[6]

- Information about copyright law must be provided to faculty, students and relevant staff members. The information is further required to explain copyright law accurately. The language of the statute is similar to a provision of the Digital Millennium Copyright Act that limits a university's liability as Online Service Provider.[7]

- Students must be notified that works used in distance education may be subject to copyright protection. Scholars suggest that a simple disclaimer or statement be included on the opening frame of the transmission.[8]

- Distance education transmissions may only be shown to students enrolled in the course and directed or supervised by the class instructor. If posted online, they must be password protected or otherwise closed to visitors outside the class.[9]

- In transmissions to remote locations or distance education, works for sale "primarily for performance or display as part of mediated instructional activities transmitted via digital networks" cannot be used. This means any materials sold to educators to use in distance education.[10]

- It is not permitted to transmit illegal copies of any works.

- Materials normally purchased by students, such as textbooks, course packs, electronic reserves, and related materials cannot be transmitted in the process of distance education.

There is nothing in the new Section 110(2) that abrogates educators' or students' rights to use works within the scope of fair use in distance education. Even works that are specifically excluded in the new procedures may still qualify for fair use and, if so, be shown or displayed in distance education. Particular attention is advised in the analysis of the fourth factor, commercial effect. Any use of works not specifically sanctioned by Section 110(2) should be considered beyond fair use if distance students are essentially supplied a substitute for a product they would normally purchase for a class.

For most colleges and universities, the materials permitted to be used in distance education will now expand beyond the parameters that existed before November 2002. But it will also require a more technical and complex process to figure out correct use of materials. Appendix D provides guidelines that may help campus administrators and faculty to comply with Section 110(2). The guidelines are based on a suggested approach by Georgia Harper from the University of Texas.[2]

Notes

1. *Distance Education: An Introduction,* Farhad Saba, Ph.D., distance-educator.com/portals/research_deintro.html
2. 17 USC Section 110(1)
3. 17 USC Section 110(2)
4. But not entire portions of audiovisual or dramatic works. You cannot defeat technological measures implemented by the rightsholder to prevent copying.
5. 17 USC Section 110(2)(A)
6. 17 USC Section 110(2)(D)(i)
7. 17 USC Section 110(2)(D)(i)
8. 17 USC Section 110(2)(D)(i)
9. 17 USC Section 110(2)(C)(i)
10. 17 USC Section 110(2)
11. *The TEACH Act Finally Becomes Law,* Georgia Harper, November 8, 2002, www.utsystem.edu/ogc/intellectualproperty/teachact.htm; *New Copyright Law for Distance Education: The Meaning and Importance of the TEACH Act,* Kenneth D. Crews, www.copyright.iupui.edu/dist_learning.htm

Chapter Eight
Copyright Policies on Campus

If knowledge can create problems, it is not through ignorance that we can solve them.
—Isaac Asimov

The use of copyright-protected materials in higher education is indispensable. The extent to which permission to use materials is sought should be a matter of college policy. For institutions seeking the limited liability protection of the Digital Millennium Copyright Act, a copyright policy and education program is mandatory.[1] A copyright policy and education program is also required for using copyright-protected materials under the new TEACH Act.[2]

A copyright policy can be established for an entire university, for a department, or for a class. However, the broader the policy, the broader the room for error and confusion. It works best to tailor guidelines with specific materials in mind. Materials for classroom assignments tend to be different than those needed to support graduate theses and dissertations; library operations may encounter yet a different set of copyright issues; and the music department another. A customized policy should be designed in the greatest detail possible regarding the type of copies required to meet the need at hand. The policy should delineate which materials require permission before copying and which ones qualify for fair use. For materials that fall somewhere in between, an educated fair use analysis should be made to determine if permission is needed, preferably by someone appointed and trained to make these analyses.

In the case of a typical classroom assignment, a set policy could permit each student to make one copy of a limited portion of an original work without obtaining permission. The same material could also be allowed to be posted online in a password-protected website that permits access to enrolled students only. Either scenario is permissible within the

scope of fair use. At the other extreme, the policy should prohibit posting copies of materials on the Internet without a password-protected site, unless permission is obtained from the rightsholder. Fair use analysis should be employed for copies that lie somewhere between the extremes.

The process for fair use analysis suggested in Chapter Five can be used in formulating copyright policy. (There are also other resources that can be found at websites referenced in this book.) The fair-use process can be written in the policy with easy, step-by-step instructions, or fair use determinations can be made in advance about specific copying needs.

> *Crafting a copyright policy requires time and resources to consider salient issues and the positions of different groups.*

There will probably always be a demand for copies that come dangerously close to or exceed the boundaries of fair use. For example, a course pack—a collection intended to serve as the assigned text for a class, which includes copies from various textbooks, journal articles, and miscellaneous sources—has been ruled to exceed fair use if the copying is conducted by a commercial business.[3] Though there has been no court opinion issued to date about the fair use standing of a course pack produced by a copy department of a nonprofit state university, a future opinion could go either way. The recommended strategy would be to get permission before proceeding.

A campus copyright policy should identify copy demand for projects, such as course packs, that would be marked for profit-making activity. These are clearly projects that the policy should allow only after permission has been obtained.

Crafting a copyright policy requires time and resources to consider salient issues and the positions of different groups. The university's legal counsel should be involved. If a policy contemplates significant budgets for staff and permission fees, the controller's office should be involved. The college's information technology or online service department also should be consulted, as more and more research and class assignments are conducted online. Since a copyright policy will affect operations for students, faculty, and staff, each of these groups also should be represented in the formulation of the policy. Policy objectives should first address the most prolific and jeopardous campus copyright problems.

Appendix E gives an example of copyright guidelines for graduate research. The guidelines are printed only as information and should not be used without competent legal advice.

Copyright Infringement and Plagiarism

Copyright infringement and plagiarism are different problems, but emulate each other. The lines of distinction between the two are not always clear. Something that constitutes copyright infringement may not necessarily constitute plagiarism. Conversely, something that constitutes plagiarism may not constitute copyright infringement. The following quote by Bruce Terry defines plagiarism and recommends how to avoid it:

Plagiarism is the presentation of another's work as your own, whether you mean to or not. Copying or paraphrasing passages from another's work without acknowledging that you've done so is plagiarism. Translating passages from another's work in another language without acknowledging that you've done so is plagiarism. Copying another writer's work without putting the material in quotation marks is plagiarism, even if credit is given. Allowing another writer to write any part of your essay is plagiarism… Plagiarism is easy to avoid. Simply acknowledge the source of any words, phrases, or ideas that you use.[4]

This advice addresses plagiarism, but not copyright infringement. One distinction between the two is that plagiarism is the use of another's work without credit, and copyright infringement is the use of another's work without permission. An-

The ideal copyright policy should be accessible and easy to locate on the campus web site, and educate the greater campus community in copyright issues.

other distinction is that plagiarism does not violate federal law; copyright infringement does. For this reason, institutions should address each issue separately.

A Comparison of Copyright Websites

There are many well-written, well-organized, university copyright websites. In order to compare a few different styles, here are some university sites—in no particular order of preference—to visit:

- www.utsystem.edu/OGC/IntellectualProperty/cprtindx.htm
- www.umuc.edu/distance/odell/cip/
- www.copyright.iupui.edu/index.htm
- www.wsu.edu/Copyright.html
- http://publications.wsu.edu/copyright/index.html
- http://fairuse.stanford.edu/
- http://depts.washington.edu/uwcopy/information/index.shtml
- www.washington.edu/faculty/facsenate/handbook/04-05-07.html
- www.indiana.edu/copyright.html
- www.lib.ncsu.edu/scc/tutorial/main.html
- www.law.cornell.edu/topics/copyright.html
- www.cis.yale.edu/grants/copyright.html
- www.usg.edu/admin/legal/copyright/
- http://toltec.lib.utk.edu/~gco/copyright.html
- www.stfrancis.edu/cid/copyrightbay/
- http://sunsite.berkeley.edu/Copyright/
- www.law.duke.edu/copyright/face/
- http://darkwing.uoregon.edu/~csundt/copyweb/
- http://scilib.ucsd.edu/howto/guides/CopyrightTips.html

A quick, random survey of university websites yields a diverse spectrum of copyright policies, from no policy whatsoever to highly progressive policies that include the application of fair use. Incredibly, many universities neglect to comply with the Digital Millennium Copyright Act (DMCA) by failing to post on their website a designated agent to receive copyright infringement claims, post a copyright policy, and provide information about copyright law as required.[5] Some universities have posted a designated agent on their website, but no policy or program for copyright education. Some have an agent and a website generally describing copyright law but no policy posted on their site. Unless in full compliance with the DMCA—by providing an agent, posting a copyright policy, and supplying information about copyright law—a university cannot qualify for the limitations in liability. The decision of whether or not to qualify for DMCA limited immunity is ultimately up to university legal counsel.

The ideal copyright policy should be accessible and easy to locate on the campus website, and educate the greater campus community in copyright issues. The policy should fully comply with the DMCA by being posted on the campus website through a link from the home page—unless legal counsel advises otherwise. It should also provide a link to a site that educates visitors generally about copyright law. If the school favors a progressive approach, the site should teach how to apply fair use analysis, providing a detailed tutorial in how to consider each of the four factors of fair use and balance the factors to determine what materials could be copied without permission. Finally, the site should provide contact information for an individual who can assist or educate others in learning and complying with copyright law.

Sovereign Immunity and Ethics

For state, nonprofit institutions, there may be a brief window of limited immunity from copyright infringement lawsuits. A federal appeals court made a decision in *Chavez v. Arte Publico Press* that states and state institutions, such as universities, are immune from copyright lawsuits that seek monetary damages.[6] The court ruled that Congress violated the 11th amendment of the U.S. Constitution by making laws that enable someone to sue a state institution for copyright or trademark infringement and seek monetary damages. What this means for anyone considering filing a lawsuit against a state university for copyright infringement is that they will likely get "poured out of court." In other words, the judge may dismiss the lawsuit based on the *Chavez* case.

The *Chavez* case is a portentous legal development. Does it mean that state universities are now free to copy whatever, whenever, with no requirement to follow copyright law? The copyright statute is *still* the law, even though a lawsuit recovering monetary damages is presently unlikely to be successful in court. It is advisable that state universities tread carefully in the matter of copyright transgressions, since there are other legal theories and remedies that could be used in court against them. Eventually, Congress may even legislate around *Chavez*, closing the loophole for good.

It is important to note that, while universities might enjoy immunity by the *Chavez* ruling, individuals on campus do not. Copyright holders may still sue individual students, faculty, and staff involved in copyright infringement. Regardless of the legal procedures, a campus copyright policy should be ethical. It should educate the campus about the law, decide where to draw the lines, and provide consequences when those lines are crossed. Copyright infringement has been compared to shoplifting. Sound ethics demand that pure infringement of intellectual property be prohibited.

Resistance to Promoting Fair Use

The copyright policies of some campuses—written or not—seem not to recognize fair use as a legitimate procedure for making copies without permission. This may be due to the doctrine's controversial nature, or because clear educational materials on the subject have been hard to find. However, there are other reasons why fair use may be difficult to promote. Commercial publishers depend on book sales to survive in a highly competitive market. In the *Kinko's* and *Michigan Document Services* cases, publishers spent a great deal on legal fees to protect their market when course packs threatened to make catalogs of academic textbooks obsolete. Publishers are not opposed to fair use per se; many publishers rely on fair use themselves in some of the works they publish. But publishers have a legitimate complaint when their products are copied for the sole reason of substituting for the purchase of their books, and many are financially prepared to legally enforce their copyrights.

The litigious and economic nature of the fair use issue makes it problematic to another group, whose professional duty is to protect their institutions from all legal claims—i.e., the legal counsel of universities. This includes state attorneys general in all state schools, as well as private firms employed by non-public institutions. Their interest in copyright law may differ from the rest of the campus. Because their mission is to protect the university from the high costs of litigation, their professional preference is typically to eliminate claims at the inception. In light of their priorities, fair use is a problematic doctrine with no guarantees, and, where there are no guarantees, no risk should be taken. Though it is inappropriate to presume any universal legal analysis, it is reasonable to recognize that some university counsels may advise against specific copy or uploading projects that might pass for fair use in a court of law. While this mission to minimize litigation is very important, it may present challenges for the teaching environment.

Time to Address Change

The need to address fair use in higher education is acknowledged by the Consortium for Educational Technology in University Systems (CETUS). CETUS is comprised of the State University of New York, the California State University System, and the City University of New York.

CETUS proclaims:

It is urgent, timely, and in the best interests of higher education that our universities raise a coordinated voice to address the topic that is known as the "fair use" of copyrighted works. The fair-use doctrine is under debate now in several different forums—locally, nationally, and internationally. The debate involves both public and proprietary interest. It arises because of the changing dynamic between the broad sweep of "intellectual properties" and the deployment of powerful and rapidly evolving communications techniques and infrastructures. These developments already have demonstrated their significant consequences for higher education and will have more pervasive effects in the future.[7]

Copyright issues on campus promise to multiply in the Digital Age. Framing a copyright policy that addresses fair use and educates all members of academe—from administration and faculty to students—is recommended to prepare for the future. Copyright law is no longer an arcane specialty to be taught only to lawyers, and it is neither practical nor cost efficient to consult a copyright lawyer about every copying decision. The evolution of education in addressing copyrights will meet with opposition. Be that as it may, it is time to consider expanding the curriculum of higher education to include copyright law to prepare for an increasingly complex future.

Notes

1. Digital Millennium Copyright Act, Section 512(e)(C)
2. Technology, Education and Copyright Harmonization Act, Section 110(2)(D)(i)
3. See the *Michigan Document Services* and *Kinko's* cases. See Chapter 4, footnote 1 and *Basic Books, Inc. v. Kinko's Graphics Corp.,* 758 F. Supp. 1522
4. Syllabi of Bruce Terry, http://ovcollege.edu/terry/sylbi106.htm
5. 17 USC 512(e)
6. *Chavez v. Arte Publico Press,* 157 F. 3rd 282 (CA 5 2000). http://laws.findlaw.com/5th/9302881cv1v3.html
7. http://www.cetus.org/fair4.html

Appendix A

When Unpublished and Published Works Pass into the Public Domain[1]

Unpublished Works

Type of Work	Copyright Term	What Became Public Domain on 1 January 2003 in the U.S.
Unpublished works	Life of the author + 70 years	Works from authors who died before 1933
Unpublished anonymous and pseudonymous works, and works made for hire (corporate authorship)	120 years from date of creation	Works created before 1883
Unpublished works created before 1978 that are published before 1 January 2003	Life of the author + 70 years or 31 December 2047, whichever is greater	Nothing. The soonest the publications can enter the public domain is 1 January 2048
Unpublished works created before 1978 that are published after 31 December 2002	Life of the author + 70 years[3]	Works of authors who died before 1933[3]
Unpublished works when the death date of the author is not known[2]	120 years from date of creation	Works created before 1883

1. Published in Peter B. Hirtle, "Recent Changes to the Copyright Law: Copyright Term Extension," *Archival Outlook,* January/ February 1999; updated 15 January 2003. Both charts are based in part on Laura N. Gasaway's chart, "When Works Pass into the Public Domain," at http://www.unc.edu/~unclng/public-d.htm, and similar charts found in Marie C. Malaro, *A Legal Primer on Managing Museum Collections* (Washington, D.C.: Smithsonian Institution Press, 1998): 155–56.

2. These works may still be copyrighted, but certification from the Copyright Office is a complete defense to any action for infringement.

3. Presumption as to the author's death requires a certified report from the Copyright Office that its records disclose nothing to indicate that the author of the work is living or died less than seventy years before.

Published Works

Time of Publication in the U.S.	Conditions	Public Domain Status
Before 1923	None	In public domain
Between 1923 and 1978	Published without a copyright notice	In public domain
Between 1978 and 1 March 1989	Published without notice, and without subsequent registration	In public domain
Between 1978 and 1 March 1989	Published without notice, but with subsequent registration	70 years after death of author, or, if work of corporate authorship, the shorter of 95 years from publication or 120 years from creation
Between 1923 and 1963	Published with notice but copyright was not renewed[1]	In public domain
Between 1923 and 1963	Published with notice and the copyright was renewed[2]	95 years after publication date
Between 1964 and 1978	Published with notice	70 years after death of author, or, if work of corporate authorship, the shorter of 95 years from publication or 120 years from creation
Between 1978 and 1 March 1989	Published with notice	70 years after death of author, or, if work of corporate authorship, the shorter of 95 years from publication or 120 years from creation
After 1 March 1989	None	70 years after death of author, or, if work of corporate authorship, the shorter of 95 years from publication or 120 years from creation

1. A 1961 Copyright Office study found that fewer than 15% of all registered copyrights were renewed. For textual material (including books), the figure was even lower: 7%.

2. A good guide to investigating the copyright and renewal status of a published work is Samuel Demas and Jennie L. Brogdon, "Determining Copyright Status for Preservation and Access: Defining Reasonable Effort," *Library Resources and Technical Services* 41:4 (October, 1997): 323–34.

Public Domain Sources

The sites listed below are intended as an alternative source for materials for use in personal websites or any other use. Materials or works in the public domain are not subject to copyright law. As such, no permission is needed before downloading. Hopefully, this one-stop-shopping list of compiled public domain sources will assist people seeking content from the Internet so they may be less likely to download materials from other sources in violation of copyright laws.

The following are sites purporting to contain databases of text, images, graphics, fonts, photos, sheet music and videos that are in the public domain. Although the materials at these sites are believed to be in the public domain, it is not possible to make that determination for all materials at the sites. Therefore they are provided with the following disclaimer:

There are no warranties, implied or otherwise, regarding:

1. **The fitness for a particular purpose of any materials or works in the respective collections of the sites ("materials or works");**

2. **The originality or accuracy of the materials or works, nor freedom from corruption either intentional or accidental; and**

3. **Compliance of copyright or other intellectual property laws by the materials or works.**

By accessing the sites compiled here, you agree to use the materials or works at these sites at your sole risk.

Text Content:

1. Books, literature – **http://promo.net/pg/index.html**
2. Books that can be read online – **http://digital.library.upenn.edu/books/**
3. Aesop's Fables – **www.pacificnet.net/~johnr/aesop/**
4. Books on the Web – **http://people.redhat.com/johnsonm/books.html**
5. Various philosophy (Plato, Aristotle, Conrad, Dostoevsky) – **www.geocities.com/Athens/Academy/3963/**
6. List of books known to be in public domain – **www.cs.indiana.edu/metastuff/bookfaq.html#8**
7. Variety of books in the public domain – **www.bartleby.com/**
8. Modern English collection – **www.hti.umich.edu/p/pd-modeng/**
9. "Jargon File" hacker slang and tradition – **www.tuxedo.org/~esr/jargon/jargon.html**
10. Archive of text to classical art songs – **www.recmusic.org/lieder/**
11. Christian classics – **www.ccel.org/**
12. Complete works of Shakespeare – **http://the-tech.mit.edu/Shakespeare/works.html**
13. Historical documents (Western Europe)* – **http://library.byu.edu/~rdh/eurodocs/**

14. Lutheran Church works("Project Wittenberg") – www.iclnet.org/pub/resources/text/wittenberg/wittenberg-home.html

15. Latin Vulgate Bible – gopher://ftp.std.com/11/obi/book/Religion/Vulgate

16. G.K. Chesterton works and biography*– www.dur.ac.uk/~dcs6mpw/gkc/index.html

17. A beginner's guide to effective email – www.webfoot.com/advice/email.top.html

Photos or Images

1. "Inexpensive" and free samples – http://www.pdimages.com/

2. Miscellaneous art clips (free) – www.clippix.com/

3. Web graphics (icons and backgrounds) – www.specialweb.com/original/

4. Government photos (animals, scenery, miscellaneous nature) – www.photolib.noaa.gov/index.html http://pictures.fws.gov/

5. Background samples – http://wp.netscape.com/assist/net_sites/bg/backgrounds.html

6. Photo archive – http://gimp-savy.com/PHOTO-ARCHIVE/

7. Clip art universe – www.nzwwa.com/mirror/clipart/

8. Celtic clip art – www.fortunecity.com/bally/tipperary/41/clipart.html

9. Inki's Clipart – www.inki.com/clipart/

10. Tornado images – www.spc.noaa.gov/faq/tornado/torscans.html

11. Images of American political history – http://teachpol.tcnj.edu/amer_pol_hist/

12. Maps[1] – www.lib.utexas.edu/maps/index.html

13. Images in the public domain – www.sru.edu/depts/cisba/compsci/dailey/public/public_domain.htm

14. Oil paintings[2] – www.1art.com/download1.htm

15. Free clipart and animations – www.barrysclipart.com/

16. Free Christmas art – www.christmasgifts.com/freeart.htm

17. Clipart for children – www.kidsdomain.com/clip/

18. Archive of art[3] – www.artchive.com/ftp_site.htm

19. Free web graphics – http://my.erinet.com/~cunning1/tiles.html

20. Pictures catalogue—National Library of Australia[4] – www.nla.gov.au/catalogue/pictures/

21. Christian clipart – www.watton.org/clipart/index.htm

22. Clipart, photos and fonts[5] – www.clip-art-center.com/

Music or Song Content:

1. www.pdinfo.com/list.htm (CDs for sale)

2. Gospel music via MP3 – http://artists.mp3s.com/artists/111/jeanne_gere.html

3. Free choral sheet music – http://www.cpdl.org/

4. Free sheet music – www.sheetmusic1.com/NEW.GREAT.MUSIC.HTML

Software Content:

1. Links to public domain software – www.stokely.com/unix.sysadm.resources/shareware.www.html

Video Content:

1. Pan American video – www.Panamvideo.com/

2. Public domain films – www.desertislandfilms.com/
   – www.retrofilm.com/

Notes

[1] Subject to conditions at: www.lib.utexas.edu/usage_statement.html
[2] Subject to the condition that copies not be used commercially.
[3] Use caution. Some of the art is still copyrighted. Copy only ancient art.
[4] Copies limited to research or education. Permission required for publication or uploading.
[5] Commercial use of any copies prohibited.

Classroom Guidelines

I. *Single Copying for Teachers*

A single copy may be made of any of the following by or for a teacher at his or her individual request for his or her scholarly research or use in teaching or preparation to teach a class:

A. A chapter from a book;

B. An article from a periodical or newspaper;

C. A short story, short essay or short poem, whether or not from a collective work;

D. A chart, graph, diagram, drawing, cartoon or picture from a book, periodical, or newspaper;

II. *Multiple Copies for Classroom Use*

Multiple copies (not to exceed in any event more than one copy per pupil in a course) may be made by or for the teacher giving the course for classroom use or discussion; *provided that:*

A. The copying meets the tests of brevity and spontaneity as defined below; *and,*

B. Meets the cumulative effect test as defined below; *and,*

C. Each copy includes a notice of copyright.

Definitions

  Brevity

  (*i*) Poetry: (a) A complete poem if less than 250 words and if printed on not more than two pages or, (b) from a longer poem, an excerpt of not more than 250 words.

  (*ii*) Prose: (a) Either a complete article, story or essay of less than 2,500 words, or (b) an excerpt from any prose work of not more than 1,000 words or 10% of the work, whichever is less, but in any event a minimum of 500 words.

  [Each of the numerical limits stated in "i" and "ii" above may be expanded to permit the completion of an unfinished line of a poem or of an unfinished prose paragraph.]

  (*iii*) Illustration: One chart, graph, diagram, drawing, cartoon or picture per book or per periodical issue.

  (*iv*) "Special" works: Certain works in poetry, prose or in "poetic prose" which often combine language with illustrations and which are intended sometimes for children and at other times for a more general audience fall short of 2,500 words in their entirety. Paragraph "ii" above notwithstanding, such "special works" may not be reproduced in their entirety; however, an excerpt comprising not more than two of the published pages of such special work and containing not more than 10% of the words found in the text thereof, may be reproduced.

  Spontaneity

  (*i*) The copying is at the instance and inspiration of the individual teacher, and (*ii*) The inspiration and decision to use the work and the moment of its use for maximum teaching effectiveness are so close in time that it would be unreasonable to expect a timely reply to a request for permission.

Cumulative Effect

(*i*) The copying of the material is for only one course in the school in which the copies are made.

(*ii*) Not more than one short poem, article, story, essay or two excerpts may be copied from the same author, nor more than three from the same collective work or periodical volume during one class term.

(*iii*) There shall not be more than nine instances of such multiple copying for one course during one class term.

[The limitations stated in "ii" and "iii" above shall not apply to current news periodicals and newspapers and current news sections of other periodicals.]

III.   *Prohibitions as to I and II Above*

Notwithstanding any of the above, the following shall be prohibited:

(A) Copying shall not be used to create or to replace or substitute for anthologies, compilations or collective works. Such replacement or substitution may occur whether copies of various works or excerpts therefrom are accumulated or reproduced and used separately.

(B) There shall be no copying of or from works intended to be "consumable" in the course of study or teaching. These include workbooks, exercises, standardized tests and test booklets and answer sheets and like consumable material.

(C) Copying shall not:

(a) substitute for the purchase of books, publishers' reprints or periodicals;

(b) be directed by higher authority;

(c) be repeated with respect to the same item by the same teacher from term to term.

(D) No charge shall be made to the student beyond the actual cost of the photocopying.

(Georgia Harper, a leading copyright scholar and manager for the Intellectual Property Section of the General Counsel for the University of Texas, developed the following to assist University of Texas faculty in applying the TEACH Act.)

Because of the many limitations, Section110(2) won't go far enough in many situations; remember that educators still have recourse to fair use to make copies, create derivative works, display and perform works publicly and distribute them to students. So don't be discouraged by Section110(2)'s scope and complexity. If it covers what you want to do and you and your institution can comply with all of its conditions and limitations, great! If it does not, you still have the fair use statute and, for University of Texas institutions, our Rules of Thumb (UT System guidelines).

So, use this handy checklist to see whether you are ready to use the TEACH Act:

❑ My institution is a nonprofit accredited educational institution or a governmental agency

❑ It has a policy on the use of copyrighted materials

❑ It provides accurate information to faculty, students and staff about copyright

❑ Its systems will not interfere with technological controls within the materials I want to use

❑ The materials I want to use are specifically for students in my class

❑ Only those students will have access to the materials

❑ The materials will be provided at my direction during the relevant lesson

❑ The materials are directly related and of material assistance to my teaching content

❑ My class is part of the regular offerings of my institution

❑ I will include a notice that the materials are protected by copyright

❑ I will use technology that reasonably limits the students' ability to retain or further distribute the materials

❑ I will make the materials available to the students only for a period of time that is relevant to the context of a class session

❑ I will store the materials on a secure server and transmit them only as permitted by this law

❑ I will not make any copies other than the one I need to make the transmission

❑ The materials are of the proper type and amount the law authorizes:

  • Entire performances of nondramatic literary and musical works

  • Reasonable and limited parts of a dramatic literary, musical, or audiovisual work

  • Displays of other works, such as images, in amounts similar to typical displays in face-to-face teaching

❑ The materials are not among those the law specifically excludes from its coverage:

• Materials specifically marketed for classroom use for digital distance education

• Copies I know or should know are illegal

• Textbooks, coursepacks, electronic reserves and similar materials typically purchased individually by the students for independent review outside the classroom or class session

❑ If I am using an analog original, I checked before digitizing it to be sure:

• I copied only the amount that I am authorized to transmit

• There is no digital copy of the work available except with technological protections that prevent my using it for the class in the way the statute authorizes

Proposed Graduate Program
Copyright Guidelines

(Provided here is an example of guidelines for graduate research. Procure competent legal advice before adopting.)

Typical Policies. Many universities, in their policy for the use of copyright-protected works as supporting materials for dissertations or theses, require copyright releases from publishers for any copyrighted material in any part of the document. Often such releases must be submitted in duplicate with the dissertation or thesis.

Acquiring permission for the use of copyright-protected materials can be very time consuming and sometimes expensive, in terms of paying permission fees. In many instances, the publisher or copyright holder cannot be located. For commercial publishers, issuing permission is generally more time consuming than permission fees are worth. What can graduate students do when it is either impossible or cost-prohibitive to get permission? Should the supporting materials be omitted altogether?

This policy ignores a vitally important copyright exception in law that is specifically intended for education and research. The Doctrine of Fair Use allows the use of limited materials for limited educational purposes without getting permission from the publisher or copyright holder. It is codified in a federal statute as Title 17, Section 107 of the Copyright Act.

As a nonprofit institution of higher education, a university should apply fair use and provide guidelines that assist students in determining when permission is necessary and when it is not. The guidelines proposed could be used to assist graduate students in making their own determination on whether attaching copies of copyright-protected work as support for their dissertation/thesis is fair use, and, if not, proceeding with the policy of obtaining permission before using copies of supporting materials.

The Fair Use Doctrine. As the proposed new guidelines on copyright for materials used in dissertations/theses rely directly on the fair use law, it is helpful to explain what the law is. Title 17, Section 107 provides:

…the fair use of a copyrighted work, including such use by reproduction by copies or phonorecords or by any other means specified by that section, for purposes such as criticism, news reporting, teaching (including multiple copies for classroom use), *scholarship or research,* is not an infringement of copyright. In determining whether the use made of a work in any particular case is fair use the factors to be considered shall include:

(1) The purpose and character of the use, including whether such use is of a commercial nature or is for nonprofit educational purposes;

(2) The nature of the copyrighted work;

(3) The amount and substantiality of the portion used in relation to the copyrighted work as a whole; and

(4) The effect upon the potential market for or value of the copyrighted work.

(Emphasis supplied)

It is not required that all four of these factors weigh in favor of fair use, but the more that do, the clearer it is that using a copy is fair use. The ultimate aim of fair use in college is to accommodate nonprofit education and research without affecting the sales of the publishers or authors who market the original work for profit. As it so happens, the vast majority of materials copied for dissertations/theses would qualify under fair use.

Copies of Materials in Support of Dissertations/Theses as Fair Use. Dissertations/theses are inherently a nonprofit, educational research function, with the sole exception of publishing the work for commercial, mass distribution. The factor that will most disqualify copies as fair use in dissertations/theses is the commercial publication of the dissertation or thesis. Doctoral dissertations are required to be published, but not all dissertations will be published commercially for mass distribution. A dissertation published in the *American Journal of Public Health*, for example, would be regarded as having been published commercially for mass distribution. Because there is a potential, however slight, that any supporting copies attached to the dissertation may intrude in the market where the originals are being sold, the supporting copies may exceed fair use parameters, thereby requiring permission to be obtained in advance. Many dissertations are published by Bell and Howell Information and Learning (formerly University Microfilms International or "UMI"). Though this is a commercial publisher, the market for these dissertations are primarily other researchers.

Publisher's Guidelines Should Apply When Dissertations/Theses are Published. When dissertations or theses are published, the publisher becomes directly involved with the issue of copyright infringement because publishers are liable for copyright infringement that occurs in their publications. Those concerns are specifically addressed in the publication agreements between the author and publisher. The publisher's copyright guidelines will be those with which a student author must comply. In the case of dissertations and theses that are submitted for publication, it follows that the graduate program should either defer to the publisher's guidelines or adopt the guidelines used by the publisher. The guidelines used by Bell and Howell Information and Learning can be accessed by visiting: www.il.proquest.com/hp/Support/Dexplorer/copyright/Part3.html.

   Since publishing a dissertation or thesis will entail a student author's compliance with the publisher's prescribed guidelines, separate guidelines are proposed for the use of supporting copies in dissertations and theses which will *not* be published outside the university system.

Proposed Guidelines for Dissertations/Theses That Will *Not* Be Published Commercially

These guidelines are for dissertations/theses that will not be published by a commercial publisher or posted on any full-access Internet site. All dissertations or theses are typically required to be archived in the university library. This does not categorize them as "commercially published." As all doctorate dissertations are required to be published, and most are published with Bell and Howell Information and Learning, these guidelines may only be adopted with the publisher's written consent. Without that consent, the publisher's guidelines must be followed, or "fair use" copies of supporting materials may be used only per publisher's consent.

1. **Supporting Copies of Copyright-Protected Materials.** There are a variety of materials that may be used in dissertations/theses as support. This includes, without limitation, text and printed media, digital content posted online, images and graphics, photos, charts and graphs, music and audio recordings, video recordings and audio-video recordings. Whether or not permission should be obtained and the extent of reproduction involved will depend on the nature of the copyright-protected materials that are used for support.

2. **When Permission Should Be Obtained.** Copying any of the following materials may not clearly qualify

as fair use and you should obtain permission or written release, or contact the university specialist in copyright law for a full analysis before you copy and attach in support of your dissertation or thesis:

a. Materials that are for sale specifically for research, educational aids, or for related scholastic activities. These materials are typically offered at retail outlets like the collegiate bookstores or online academic services sites. Also included are photos or images on websites hosted by a commercial operation that offers the photos and images for sale;

b. Materials which have not already been commercially published. This includes student papers, other unpublished dissertations or theses, articles or essays by professors that are posted on university password-protected web sites. It does not include any materials posted on a full-access web site;

c. Articles, treatises, essays or other print media that are copied and attached in entirety to the dissertation or thesis;

d. Forms such as surveys, job applications, tests, or any prepared document that requires information to be filled in on blank lines;

e. Songs or audio tracks, including anything recorded by tape, CD or DVD;

f. Videotapes, cassettes, or DVDs;

g. Software;

h. Separate or individual blueprints, architectural designs, or schematics that are not published in a group of several designs in a book, article, or journal;

i. Fictional works like poetry, short stories, novels, and plays;

j. Entertainment art or graphics, such as cartoons and paintings;

k. Sculpture, such as carved wood, stone, bone, ceramic, porcelain or similar materials.

3. **When Permission Is Not Required.** Fair use requires that only a portion of an original work be copied. However, there may be supporting materials that will need to be copied in their entirety, such as photos, single frame images, and the like. As long as the dissertation or thesis is not commercially published, it is permitted to copy without permission whole portions of such materials. Otherwise, there are no hard limits on how much of an original can be copied without permission. As a general rule, however, only enough of the original should be copied to support the proposition. It must be something less than the whole original. Unless otherwise noted, the following may be copied, as long as it is only a *portion* of the original:

a. Nonfiction printed and published materials—books (including textbooks), articles, treatises, essays, and dissertations—to name a few examples;

b. Digital content posted on a website, except when the host or author expressly forbids downloading without permission;

c. Entire portions of photographs, scientific graphs, charts, x-rays, seismographic and related measurements made by devices, and graphic images that are purely scientific in nature;

d. Entire blueprints, architectural designs, or schematics that are published in a book, article, or journal with several other such designs, as long as the entire book or article is not copied;

e. Entire quotes from famous people;

f. Fictional works, such as poetry, short stories, novels, or plays—but only if a few lines or sentences from each are used;

g. All copyright-protected materials that were published before 1923. Those copyrights have expired. These may be copied in their entirety.

4. **No Connection to or Association with Profit-making or Commercial Activities.** At no time can copies be used in connection with any activities that have a profit-making or commercial purpose. This would include selling a dissertation or thesis, or giving copies to someone else who might sell or otherwise earn money from the copies. Other than as part of a resume, it is not permitted to use a dissertation or thesis containing supporting copies of others' works in any way in relation to a job with a commercial business or company.

5. **All Other Copies for Supporting Materials.** Any other copies of materials under consideration to use as supporting material that are not covered under these guidelines should be submitted for fair use analysis to a copyright lawyer or other person well educated in copyright law.